ENGAGING ECCENTRICS

DAVID HERBERT

ENGAGING ECCENTRICS

RECOLLECTIONS

PETER OWEN · LONDON

For my nephew Henry Pembroke,
who through his affection and kindness has made
me feel Wilton is still my home

PETER OWEN PUBLISHERS
73 Kenway Road London SW5 0RE

First published in Great Britain 1990
© David Herbert 1990

British Library Cataloguing in Publication Data
Herbert, David, *1908–*
Engaging eccentrics: recollections.
1. Morocco. Herbert, David, 1908–
I. Title
964.04092

ISBN 0–7206–0788–4

Photoset by Rowland Phototypesetting Ltd
Bury St Edmunds Suffolk
Printed in Great Britain by Billings of Worcester

CONTENTS

ILLUSTRATIONS

PART ONE

Tangier 1978

My birthday had arrived yet again. It was a lovely October morning and still warm enough for me to have breakfast in my dressing-gown on the terrace. I was enjoying myself, eating scrambled eggs and bacon and giving my three cats, Essex, Dudley and Lady Jane Grey, their saucers of bread and milk. I thought how lucky I was to have such a pleasant, carefree life. I felt happy and warmed by the morning mail which had brought letters and birthday cards from my many friends and relatives. I was indulging in lazy contemplation of how delightful the world was if you took no active part in trying to run it when I was interrupted by my servant, Mustafa, telling me that the electric-light man had come to read the meter.

'What a nuisance,' I said. 'Do they want to be paid now or can I send them a cheque?'

'Now,' he said.

So I went upstairs to get my cheque-book. It wasn't where I expected it to be. I looked for it in all the most unlikely places and eventually found it in the inside pocket of a tweed jacket that I had not worn for several days. By this time the breakfast hour of peace had vanished; so had the rest of my scrambled eggs and bacon. The cats beamed contentedly. I didn't. The sun had disappeared behind a cloud and the coffee was cold!

I then moved to do the daily chores of running a house and garden which I do every morning before getting dressed.

I wake up at once in the mornings – no snoozing. I am at my best and pull back the curtains, eager to see whether the sun is shining. It usually is here, but if it is not, I think: rain, perhaps. How wonderful for the garden. I put on my dressing-gown and the first thing I do is to go and see if my birds are alive and well. It is always a worrying moment, as often, for no apparent reason, a bird has fallen from its perch in the aviary and is dead. Yesterday I found one of my beautiful green and black parrots with red legs and blue wings face downwards, floating in the bird-bath. I am sure it is not the cold, and I am beginning to think it comes from constipation. Their excrement gets stuck to the feathers and forms a hard crust. When they are flying around in a large aviary, there is no way of knowing whether this has occurred. One would have to catch them each morning and wash their bottoms, an impossible task, and anyway they would probably die of fright if one tried to do so.

My next move is to walk slowly around the garden to see what flowers have come out and which ones have withered. I take my secateurs with me and snip off the dead heads; then I start picking flowers for the house, but only where it will not be noticed – a few here, a few there. It is a pity to ruin the garden to beautify the house. So many non-gardeners remorselessly cut great branches from some lovely shrub and leave a gaping scar.

Gardening is a rewarding hobby. There is always something that needs tending, especially in this climate, in which there is never a non-growing period. For instance, in May some nasty black beetles appear and creep into the centres of any flower that is white or yellow. They start eating from inside outwards, so unless you are aware of their existence and prise them out with the point of a pair of scissors, the flower is ruined. They particularly like white roses.

The Moroccans know how to arrange flowers. They have a different approach to others in the way they mix their bouquets. The flower market is an exquisite sample of this – not just bunches tied together with string, but delicate arrangements of contrasting coloured blooms with a circle of evergreen leaves around them. Moroccans use flowers in a completely individual way. We are apt to arrange just a bowl of roses – lovely, but with no originality. They put a rose here and a rose there, mixed with any other flower available. The result is like a Persian painting. Their arrangements can also be architectural; they put incredible colours together and often the final effect is like a minaret, a pagoda or a pyramid. They have a great feeling for flowers. Often along the roads you see Moroccan men and women carrying a simple rose or a little bunch of wild flowers. At their own parties they will spend hours pinning individual flowers on to the skirt of a table-cloth, totally obliterating the material.

In the early spring when it is still cold, if a single blossom comes out on a fruit tree the Moroccans say the tree is dreaming. This is a charming thought and typical of the poetry in them. During that season too, jasmine, wisteria, bridal wreath and Judas trees are in full bloom, and the scent of the two former plants through the house and garden is intoxicating. From this moment on, there is never a dull moment. Each day some new plant or shrub comes out. This continues all through the summer until the end of the September, if you are lavish with your watering.

Many groups of gardening friends and botanists have visited my garden. When they arrived I feel much less worried about the weather, as for them the early spring bulbs, narcissus, iris and other winter flowers make up for the lack of sun. Not so with ordinary visitors, for the fickleness of the weather in Tangier is famous. My heart sinks if they come in January or February and I am forced to drive hundreds of miles in search of the sun.

I am such a lover of birds that I am sure I was a bird in my former life. I have aviaries in the garden and mix all types together – finches, parrots, canaries, cardinals, budgerigars, silver and golden pheasants. All seem to get on well. They give me great pleasure. I was especially fond of my minah bird, known as Morris Minor. He was never caged and followed me everywhere. He talked incessantly and sang the Raspeil when particularly happy. One day I came home to find Antonio, my cook, in tears. Morris had seen a succulent grub in one of the wells and had flown down to catch it, landing on the water, but apparently he had been unable to rise again. Too late, he was dead. I was miserable. Antonio told me he had tried artificial respiration by moving his wings back and forth. That, at least, made me smile. Then I asked where he was. 'In the fridge,' he replied.

I had a small white and yellow cockatoo which I bought in Lisbon. I drove back to Tangier with Patata Frita perched on my shoulder. He had only one eye and a deformed leg but was a fascinating bird. Six months later I went to England. When I returned he would not speak to me, but screeched and ruffled up his feathers whenever I approached him. He hated me, perhaps because I had left him or perhaps someone had teased him in my absence. Anyway, try as I could, we were never friends again.

My latest friend in the bird world is a silver pheasant. He makes charming cooing noises whenever he sees me, eats out of my hand, and at the least opportunity flies on to my head. He is very heavy and his claws are extremely sharp, but I dare not move him, so I wait patiently until he decides to move. He has killed two wives, but is kindly to the other birds in the aviary.

Creating a house, a way of life, an environment, gives me a feeling of fulfilment, which over the years I have shared with my family and my friends who have repeatedly visited me. I have travelled all over Morocco with them countless times, enchanted journeys, journeys of which I never tire, always to the same places, but each time with a different experience.

I like entertaining and I invite a great many people to my house, either for luncheon or dinner, but in the forty years I have lived here I have not given a cocktail party. It is a form of entertainment I do not enjoy. Either you are stuck with someone you don't like, or, if you are talking to someone you do like, you are sure to be interrupted. Apart from that, it is no place to have real conversation. Usually the person whose attention you are trying to hold is looking past you to see who else is in the room. Also, I have the feeling that the host and hostess are returning hospitality by inviting all the people who have entertained them in the past six months in the cheapest and easiest manner. Generally the heat is terrific, the noise intolerable. Moreover, your eyes smart for several hours after you have left, thanks to the dense fog of cigarette-smoke to which you have been subjected.

The form of entertaining I enjoy is to have a dozen or more friends to dinner or lunch. If you take the trouble to place people who are congenial next to each other, irrespective of rank, the party should turn out pleasantly. In Tangier, where so many different languages are spoken, it is essential to place people according to who talks what. If you don't, there are sure to be yawning silences, boredom written on the faces of the guests. Naturally, if the meal is official, then you have to place people properly and prepare yourself for a stuffy, maybe tedious evening.

Every birthday encourages a certain introspection, a wish to make a sort of balance sheet of one's life. Like most people, I ask myself the question, 'Have I led the kind of life I wanted? If I could start again, would I choose the life I have led, the life I lead?' I think my answer is 'Yes', for from the moment I decided to leave England and live here, where else but Tangier could have developed to the same extent my tastes, my hopes and indeed the very concept of my life?

As a young man I wished to be an actor. I have already recounted in *Second Son* the fate of my aspirations and I am convinced that, on the boards, I should have been just one more performer. However, in the life which I chose to lead in Tangier, I believe that I have played the part of an actor as well as that of director and puppet manager. No other town could have fulfilled my purpose to the same extent. Over the years, Tangier has been visited by a continuous stream of the most varied, outstanding, eccentric, engaging people imaginable – artists, writers, actors, political and social figures. I entertained all of them, and have brought many kindred souls together. In the following pages I shall try to evoke the memory of some encounters with both passing visitors and local personalities. The role in which I cast myself implied not only a definite taste for entertaining and social life, but also the need to create around myself an agreeable atmosphere and to make my house a place where every man, myself included, feels at ease, relaxed and receptive.

As it happened, I did not really choose my own house. I decided to make my home in Morocco in 1949. There were several reasons for my decision. Before the Second World War the house in which I now live had been left to me in the will of a remarkable spinster, Jessie Green. She was half English and half Romanian, her mother being a member of the Titulescu family. In those days Jessie was comfortably off, but after the war she lost nearly everything, owing to the Russian take-over of Romania. In 1946 she wrote that unless I came out to Tangier at once, and rented her house while arranging to build a smaller one for her in the garden, she would be forced to sell it. This letter was just the right push I needed.

Going back to my house in the Park at Wilton after the war was like going back to school. Mothers and fathers seldom realize when their children are no longer children. I was not allowed a key to the Lodge Gates. As they were locked at 10 p.m., my comings and goings at night were made impossible. My father was no longer young and he was not well. He was the kindest of men, but dominated by my mother, and rather than have an argument, he agreed with everything she said or did. I felt that he would not live much longer and, though fond of my elder brother, I knew that living in the Park under his tenure would, or could, be worse than under my mother's. They were much alike in character. As long as my father was alive, Wilton was my home, but on the succession of my brother it would cease to be my home in the same way.

I decided to do as Jessie wished. I built her the small house she craved and took possession of her old one. I made alterations, decorated it, and in my own way re-created a typically English environment where my furniture, pictures, drawings and objects all easily found their own place. Subsequently I attacked the garden, which I laid out carefully and with love, building large, hospitable cages for my birds.

In my garden there are some cement steps descending from one terrace to the other. These steps were put there by Jessie Green when I built her the smaller house in the garden. They were made by a workman who was practically blind and remarkably stupid, but cheap. He was also large and ugly. Being unable to see, he walked on the top step before the cement was dry, but only with one foot. He was about to erase the footprint when Jessie shouted from the verandah. 'No, no, don't let him touch it!'

'Why?' I asked.

'Because I like it like that. I shall call it the Mark of the Beast.'

Jessie had a faithful retainer, Aicha, who had worked for her for thirty years. Her English was impeccable; so good was it that on the telephone nobody knew whether it was Jessie or Aicha. I was always saying, 'Good morning, darling.' 'It's Aicha, Mr David.' Or 'Good morning, Aicha, may I speak to the Señorita?' 'It's not Aicha, it's me.' Jessie enjoyed it, as she could pretend she was Aicha whenever she didn't want to speak to someone.

There was a love-hate relationship between them, and Aicha gave Jessie as good as she got. Answering back in the same tone as Jessie, she would say things like, 'Miss Jessie, you will never go to

Heaven if you talk to me like that.' 'I don't want to go to Heaven,' Jessie would reply. 'Well, Miss Jessie, the best place for you is under the sod.'

Jessie disliked her neighbour who lived in a house across the lane. He was a Moroccan and a plumber, and as far as I was concerned, a nice man. Why Jessie took against him, I shall never know. Jessie, if she developed a dislike of someone, was merciless; she would torment that person in any way she could. Her form of torture of the poor plumber was to put her two noisy parrots on their perches as near as possible to the dividing hedge. They screamed all day and most of the night. The plumber first complained, then pleaded, and eventually came to me begging me to intervene with Jessie on his behalf. He said his wife was not well and could not sleep. 'Nonsense,' said Jessie. 'When I approached, I saw her in the lane yesterday.' And she continued her torture.

The plumber won in the end. How he managed to poison the parrots I don't know, but one morning Jessie said, 'One of my parrots is dead.'

'Really,' I said. 'How extraordinary – it was perfectly well yesterday.'

Two days elapsed and the other one died. Jessie was miserable, but would never admit that they had been killed by the plumber. However, I am sure they were, because when I saw him two weeks later walking with his wife in the village, he said, with a twinkle, 'Mr David, how kind of Miss Jessie to move her parrots. She must have moved them a very long way away, as we don't hear them at all now.'

Just before the war Mr Keeling was our Minister at the Legation. His wife Magda was Italian. She was pro-Axis and had nothing in common with the English community. She even sent our official invitations to the Legation written in French. As far as Jessie was concerned, that was the last straw. So, in reply to one of the gold embossed invitations, she wrote: 'Miss Verte is very triste that she cannot accept the kind invitation, parce que elle talk no français.'

From then on the invitations were written in English.

Madame de Marrange, an American lady, widow of a French count, bought a house here and lived in a pretentious way – the footmen wore white gloves, and all the other trimmings of the *nouveaux riches* were much in evidence. She told a great friend of Jessie's, who lived in Rome, that Jessie was *déclassée* in Tangier because she sat at bar-stools and consorted with barmen. Jessie was furious and wrote to the Countess:

> Dear Mrs Marrange
>
> I have received a letter from my friend, Julia Bambini, telling me that you say I am *déclassée*. Thank you. At least you admit I was once *classée*. I don't know where you came from, or if you were ever *classée*, but I do know that you are a newcomer here whom I have fortunately not had the pleasure to meet. I am told your footmen wear white cotton gloves, which I must inform you are not only out of date, but very *déclassée*.
>
> Jessie Green

Jessie walked with two sticks, and over the years it had been her privilege to park her car in the courtyard of the Legation. An unpleasant new Minister arrived and sent a message that in the future Miss Green must not park her car in the courtyard. The next time that Jessie was invited, she blew her horn loudly, shot through the gates and drove her car straight on to the newly mown lawn. 'After all,' said Jessie, 'they only mentioned the courtyard.'

In future she used the courtyard.

Many people considered Jessie a snob. She was not, and she once explained to me why certain people considered her so. Jessie was an old lady not far off ninety, so she had lived in Tangier from around the 1880s. Her uncle was the Minister at that time. She had known families who, when she was a girl, used the back door of the Legation. Over the years they had prospered and become members of so-called 'society'. When I first came here, there were two beautiful women, well married, and invited everywhere. Jessie had known them as children; their father had been the plumber, and their mother her aunt's lady's maid. 'It is difficult for me to treat them quite as my equals, for every time I go to the loo, I see their father's name on the lavatory pan.'

There still exist descendants of other families of the same humble origin, but by now all that is forgotten and in many cases not even known. But for Jessie, who if she were alive today would be ninety-seven or ninety-eight, it would still seem like yesterday, so it is understandable that in certain circles she was thought snobbish.

Jessie was a law unto herself. She rode roughshod over policemen, governors, ministers, in fact anyone in authority who got in her way. She obtained a special pass from the Head of Police, allowing her to park her car wherever she liked. She took advantage of this by purposely parking it in impossible places, thereby obstructing traffic. Some years before she died, the Head of Police was replaced, so Jessie's permit became invalid. She continued, however, to behave in the same way. Most of the policemen knew her and turned a blind eye, but eventually there were so many complaints from other drivers that Jessie was arrested several times and given a fine.

On one occasion Jessie flared up and said in Arabic, 'How dare you arrest me and tell me what and what not to do! I am the daughter of the Bashador [Ambassador].'

'No, Miss Jessie,' said the policeman. 'You are not his daughter, you are his niece, and he was not Bashador anyway, but only Minister.'

'Touché,' said Jessie, and paid the fine.

I am glad that she died when she did. She could never have adapted herself to the new Morocco, a go-ahead country, totally independent, with no need of Europeans. Jessie loved the Moroccans. She understood them and they her, but she had that feeling of superiority which so many English people in so many parts of the world have had since the start of the British Empire. Now, most Europeans with a grain of intelligence have abandoned such attitudes.

Jessie told me that years ago, in the early part of the century, a British liner was wrecked off Cap Spartel. Minor members of the British royal family were amongst the passengers – I believe the Duke and Duchess of Fife, Princess Helena Victoria and Princess Marie Louise. All the passengers were saved, but none of the luggage. Jessie said that for many years on that wild, isolated coast, the Moroccan men and women were seen wearing spangled evening dresses, feather boas, black satin shoes with *diamanté* buckles, and carrying ostrich-feather fans.

The telephone system in Tangier leaves a lot to be desired and over the years has been the cause of many jokes. At moments the lines get crossed. One day you hear your neighbour talking to another friend and hastily ring off thinking, Good God, what did I say to so and so about so and so – I hope I wasn't overheard. The worst case of this was when I picked up the telephone and heard my old friend Jessie Green talking to Bob Lebus, who had a house close by. The following conversation ensued:

'Good morning, Jessie darling. Did you have a nice evening at David's last night?'

'No. Filthy dinner, rotten company, and everybody left at ten-thirty.'

'Oh Jessie, how extraordinary. Usually David's parties are such fun,' replied Bob.

I rang off and went around to Jessie, who lived next door. 'Good morning,' I said. 'Sorry you had such a filthy dinner last night.'

'Darling, it was delicious.'

'Sorry the people were so uncongenial.'

'But they were charming.'

'How strange. You see, I've just heard your conversation with Bob.'

Silence. For once I had got the better of the formidable Jessie, and I then continued: 'You were very cantankerous last night. Incidentally, darling, after we had dropped you home, we all returned to my house and had a wonderful evening lasting until two-thirty.'

I tell this story to all newcomers as a warning to be careful with their telephone conversations!

PART TWO

I first came to Tangier in 1933 with a party of young friends, Poppet John, the daughter of Augustus John, Reine Pitman, John Singer Sargent's niece, and my cousin, Michael Duff. It was a wonderful trip. From then on I was drawn to Morocco. I visited it several times up to 1939, when the Second World War started, and I didn't return again until 1946, when I decided to live in Tangier permanently. So now it is over thirty years that I have been a resident here. Many of my friends and acquaintances during those early years have since died, so I think it is only right to start my reminiscences about them.

One of the first people Jessie Green introduced me to was Jack Sinclair, who at first looked fierce. He resembled a great black bird of prey. Exceptionally, tall, dark skinned, and with an eagle's beak for a nose, he was a splendid figure. In actual fact he was totally unlike his appearance, being a gentle, kind character. He had been Governor of Zanzibar for many years. He was also a good architect and designed many public buildings there. When he retired to Tangier, he built four houses, one for himself and his wife, Muriel, one for his daughter, Jackie, and one for each of his two grand-daughters, Sally and Tessa. Jack organized the polo here, ran the Country Club, and amongst other pursuits gave Sunday afternoon croquet parties. These resembled a Sunday afternoon in England – plates of curled-up ham sandwiches, tepid tea, jugs of warm orange-juice in which many ants could be found bathing, and dishes of strawberries and cream. The parties started at 4 p.m. and usually lasted until 7.30 p.m., when, after strenuous games of croquet on a very uneven lawn, we would be given a stiff whisky and soda and sent home. His beautiful but, to say the least, eccentric wife Muriel would stand on the veranda as the guests arrived, dressed in some flowing garment, usually with a mug of something in her hand, hurling insults at you if you were lucky, heavy silver ornaments if you were not. When she particularly wished to annoy her patient husband, she would leap astride her horse and canter happily through Tangier in her nightgown. This behaviour naturally upset poor Jack, who was highly thought of and a very respectable member of the British community.

Of the three granddaughters, Jane, the eldest, is the stablest of the family. She is a tall, fair-skinned, beautiful, conventional girl, happily married to a rosy cheeked, fox-hunting squire. The second, Sally, who was killed in a riding accident, was a golden-eyed, sultry charmer. She was adventurous and gay; had she lived, she would certainly have become somebody of immense interest. Tessa, the youngest, resembles an exquisite, undernourished Persian boy. She is willowy, flat-chested, doe-eyed, and laughs the way a donkey brays. She is as unconventional as her sister is conventional. She likes to shock. Although full of talent, she is unable to stick to anything she starts. Some of her photographs of women are dreams of beauty, romantic and touching; others are hard, severe and cruel, but equally brilliant in their conception. At the start of any venture, the enthusiasm is terrific, but fades quickly as some other idea enters her head.

At that earlier period Tessa was in love with being in love, and was apt to think of herself as an extra in *The Wilder Shores of Love*, Lesley Blanch's fascinating portrayal of eccentric European ladies. Tessa was much more sensitive than she wished the world to believe, so she contradicted one whenever possible, dressed wilfully and badly. However, when she took the trouble, she staggered one with her exceptional beauty. Tessa is now happily married to a tycoon named Stuart Wheeler, and has three lovely daughters ranging from nine years old to three.

Miss Drummond Hay, an Edwardian, still dressed in the same style as when she grew up. A botanist of some renown, she lived in Tangier half the year in a house not far from mine. She would go on long expeditions in the Rif Mountains entirely by herself, and come back joyfully carrying a plastic bag full of rare wild flowers. I remember once going to Ketama with Jamie Caffery and the Dunlops. Harry Dunlop was the doctor here, and his wife Teddy was Vice-Consul at our Legation. We found Miss Drummond Hay in the same hotel as ourselves. She was leaving early in the morning on foot to climb the mountain behind the hotel where she had been told by someone that she might find the wild yellow tulip. The sun was blazing and off she went by herself, dressed as for a garden party, and we did not see her until dinner. When we came down to the dining-room and went to our table, there lay a little bunch of wild flowers on each of our plates. They were quite wilted. Teddy said, 'Really, this hotel, laying dead flowers on the table.' She was about to throw them away when I said, 'Perhaps they are a token of esteem to you two botanists from Miss Drummond Hay.'

I was right. She sailed into the room, crossed to our table and told us the name of each wilted flower.

She was very proud of her complexion, so I thought it strange that she should walk all day in the burning sun without a parasol. Oddly enough she was carrying one when she came in to dinner. Afterwards she said, 'Now I am going for my evening moonlight walk.' Up went the parasol. Not unnaturally, we all looked rather surprised. Miss Drummond Hay turned to us and said, 'The world is wrong about the sun's rays being harmful. It's the moon's rays that are the wicked ones. That is why at night I always carry my paralune.'

Lady Tweeddale emigrated to Tangier about fourteen years ago. She had spent a quarter of a century at Yester in Scotland, the Tweeddale family home. Lord Tweeddale was very ill for the last five years of his life and Marjorie rarely moved from Scotland. When eventually he died, the house, after having been in the family for so many centuries, was sold by the trustees. Marjorie was miserable and could not bear to leave, so she rented it from the purchasers on a yearly basis. This arrangement hadn't worked. Sadly, she decided to leave Scotland and try to make a new life in England, but her heart was not in it. Having been away so long, she had lost most of her friends. All her children by her first marriage were married with grown-up children. She bought a house in

Gloucestershire, but she never really liked it. She felt lonely, as her neighbours were, on the whole, unwelcoming.

One year her sister, Viv Starling, asked if she might bring her to stay. She came, loved Tangier, and everybody liked her. She decided to rent a house for six months to see whether she wished to live here permanently. She did, and bought a delightful house not far from mine on the Mountain. She was completely happy, entertained charmingly and made many friends. Her children and grandchildren visited her continually. She was a great asset to the community, and joined all the local charities, which reminded her of the days at Yester where she had worked indefatigably for so many years. It is remarkable that a woman of her age was able to uproot herself, say farewell to England, and settle down so serenely in Morocco. She never had any regrets, and told me that after being in England three weeks, she would count the days until her return.

When I first met Marjorie she was not forthcoming and had little to say. Later she told me that as a girl her mother bullied her and said, 'The trouble with you is you have no small talk, or large talk either.' This, not surprisingly, gave Marjorie an inferiority complex, but it fast disappeared.

Tangier has this effect on many people I have known, who arrive here timid and unsure of themselves. Later on they have blossomed. This is due, I think, to the warmness of the Moroccans themselves, and the peculiar type of European who has made his or her home here. They want to like people, and will open their arms to welcome a newcomer. You have to blot your copy-book very heavily to be cold-shouldered. It is the most tolerant of places.

Lady Tweeddale inspired a great feeling of friendship. She was a perfect hostess, a sympathetic and charming friend. When she died recently, she left a great void. I remember with admiration and devotion her serenity during the last month of her life. A few days before the end, she was still receiving her intimate friends for lunch or dinner. She was extremely weak, but her will was so strong that she was able to join in the conversation from her bed. When you went into her bedroom, you could not believe she was about to die, as she was still beautifully turned out, with her hair well done, her face well made up, her pearls around her neck, her nails manicured, surrounded by lace pillows and vases of flowers from her garden that she loved so much. She never spoke about her illness and never lost her sense of humour.

When it rains here, it rains with a vengeance. Christmas and New Year 1976–7 were certainly the worst winter I have ever experienced in all the years I have lived in Tangier. Old houses such as mine have flat roofs, and that winter the rain was so heavy that the drain-pipes were unable to carry away the water fast enough, so that at one moment it was a foot deep on my roof. No roof can stand that for long, and after the first week the water came pouring through into my drawing-room. So we lived with rows of buckets spaced strategically across the floor to catch the worst cascades.

Marjorie and I decided to go to Meknes to see a friend, Hamid Nuamani. We started off in high spirits, not realizing the state of the roads. The trip was disastrous; we took nine hours to reach Meknes instead of two and a half. We drove through rivers of water at Larache, the road over the salt flats having completely disappeared. If it had not been for the avenue of lorries and charabancs on each side of where the road was, we should not have been able to identify it. These stranded vehicles had tried to define the road in the dark, but had missed it and had toppled over into the flooded salt flats. A group of tourists in a smart Volvo coach were sitting up to their ankles in water. The engine, higher than the passenger seats, was not affected, and the driver, who was separated from the main coach, ploughed on through the floods at far too great a speed, without thought for the people who were paying for this unpleasant trip.

We eventually were diverted and reached higher ground in a lonely but lovely part of the country. Suddenly the car stopped, and we realized that water must have got into the petrol tank. Nobody was in sight, and there were no garages within miles. So we waited hoping that someone would pass by.

After a quarter of an hour a car appeared and stopped. A friendly, good-looking Moroccan asked if he could help. We discovered that he managed some of the King's farms, including one nearby. He left us and returned with a rope and station-wagon, and towed us to the farm, where he had mechanics waiting to work on our car. The farmhouse, yard and outbuildings were lovely, and while waiting we were shown an extraordinary sight. There were four thousand lambs, all of the same age, separated from their mothers during the day and fed on pellets. At night they were returned to their mothers to drink their milk. At four months they are killed and exported as *agneaux de lait*. It sounds cruel, but they seemed happy enough skipping around and playing games with each other, oblivious of their fate.

We were given mint tea and biscuits. It was then two o'clock, and we still had some distance to go before reaching Meknes. We had left Tangier at seven that morning.

Ira Belline, to whom I dedicated *Second Son*, and who played a great part in my life in Tangier, once told me how it happened that she came to Morocco. During the last month of the Second World War Ira, Jay Haselwood and Bill Chase met while working for the American Red Cross in Marseilles. Ira, a niece of Stravinsky, had been in hiding ever since the Nazis invaded France. A White Russian allowed to live in France, she had no legal papers. The two men were American. When the American Red Cross in that area became redundant, the three of them decided to stay together, sail to North Africa and try to start a business – a restaurant, small hotel, bar or night-club. They landed at Casablanca. None of them had much money, but I imagine they had saved a certain amount or they would not have undertaken this adventurous journey with such optimism. After a short time, however, they discovered that life was not as cheap as they had been led to believe, and that quite a large capital sum was required to start any form of business.

One day they were sitting disconsolately in a street café in Rabat, when they noticed a large, expensive, chauffeur-driven car cruising backwards and forwards past them. They were much intrigued by its occupant, a fair-haired, flamboyant woman wearing outsize black spectacles. On her shoulder was perched a white and yellow cockatoo, while crawling all over her were a dozen or more hairless dogs. Several larger breeds sat or rather romped about beside the unfortunate chauffeur. Eventually the car stopped. The woman emerged in jodphurs, the cockatoo still on her shoulder, followed by her indecent-looking, yapping entourage. She walked straight to the table and said in a deep, husky voice, 'I hope you will excuse me, but I have come to tell you that I consider you the three most attractive human beings I have ever seen. Will you come to dinner? It is now twelve noon. I will give you till seven o'clock to reflect. If you decide to accept my invitation, meet me at the bar of the Tour Hassan Hotel.' With that, she walked away without a word of farewell or even a backward glance.

They were all three stunned. Ira recovered first and said, 'Do you realize that no one took the slightest notice of her? Imagine, a bird on her shoulder and surrounded by her dozen dogs, yet she caused no sensation. She must be a well-known figure here.'

They spent an hour or more discussing this mysterious woman. Was she mad or drunk? Would she really be at the Tour Hassan that evening? Did she intend to give them dinner or had she already forgotten their existence? Eventually they decided that they had nothing to lose and agreed to go to the rendezvous.

Bill suddenly said, 'But what if she isn't there when we arrive? We can't just sit without ordering a drink. And drinks are expensive, if you remember the first night we got here. Incidentally, since I'm in charge of the cash, I think I should tell you we're practically broke.'

Ira shrugged her shoulders and Jay said, 'What the hell. Let's risk it.'

Not to appear too eager (if indeed the unknown woman was really there), they arrived at 7.30 p.m. and entered the hotel with trepidation. Ira, in her grandest manner, said, 'Which way to the bar?' 'The end of the hall, madame, then to your left.'

As they drew nearer, their spirits rose, for they heard the unmistakable yapping of those naked little ratlike dogs. Sure enough, there the woman sat with the cockatoo still on her shoulder, but she had also brought two Afghan hounds and a blue macaw, which was contentedly eating the back of a chair.

'So you've come. I thought you would. Have a drink – have two drinks. I've had four. Now tell me your names – Ira, Jay and Bill. That's fine. What are you doing here? Nothing – I see. No money, from the looks of you. That's a pity if you want to stay in Morocco. You want to start a restaurant in Tangier, do you? Plenty of room for another restaurant there. Incidentally, I have a large house just outside the town. You can stay there if you like while looking for suitable premises.'

And so the conversation went on. Drink after drink was brought to the table, and by the time their hostess decided it was dinnertime, Ira was the only sober member of the party.

They drove to a property on the Casablanca road. Only on their arrival did they learn that their hostess was the Comtesse de la Faille – half American, half Scottish, married to a Belgian, an eccentric lady whose passion for animals, birds and so forth was such that she had no idea how many she owned. Horses, donkeys, mules, dogs, cats, desert rats, foxes wandered around the property. Aviaries and aquariums teeming with rare birds and tropical fish were planted strategically in the garden. But her eccentricity went just so far, for she knew perfectly well which were the valuable beasts. They were cared for with greater diligence, and kept on chairs or in kennels.

Phyllis was not disappointed by her 'pick-ups', and put up enough money for them to rent premises in Tangier suitable for a high-grade restaurant. She also paid for the new kitchens and washrooms, and for complete redecorating and furnishings. Ira and Jay had exceptionally good taste, and on the opening night the décor was much admired. They named it the Parade, and the first night was a social and gastronomic success. Many well-known people attended, including Diana Cooper, Paul-Louis Weiller, Barbara Hutton, Drian, the French painter, and the James McBeys.

The restaurant thrived for several years, but there came a falling-out between the three partners. Ira was the first to leave. She disagreed with Bill over the running of the business. Then Bill left because Phyllis, who was still the virtual owner, fell in love with Jay. She ignored Bill and in any argument sided against him. The restaurant closed.

Ira opened an unsuccessful flower shop. Bill left for the West Indies, and Jay became gigolo to the Countess. As Jay had a marked preference for boys, Charles de la Faille was not unduly disturbed. He considered his wife in perfectly safe hands.

Six months later the Parade reopened in the Rue des Vignes with Jay in charge. Until 1982 it continued to be run by Lily Wykman, a French woman married to a Swede. She became Jay's great friend and partner. When he died, she had inherited the restaurant.

Ira, Bill and Jay are all dead, and the widowed Phyllis lived in a wheelchair surrounded by her animals somewhere near Lisbon until she died recently.

Lily Wykman, the owner of the Parade Bar, was French. She was petite, and though no longer young, she remained pretty. Her eyes were heavily painted and smudged like a Marie Laurencin painting, and her hair was cut like a poodle. She dressed well and wore a great deal of costume jewellery. She started life in a circus; her father, I believe, being the proprietor. I knew her long before the days of the Parade Bar. She had toiled at many strangely assorted jobs, and her life had been far from easy. At last she was established and no longer had to worry as to where the next penny was coming from. Her husband died some time ago and her mother a short while back. Her stepdaughter lives in Sweden, so Lily had no more responsibilities except the restaurant, where she was indefatigable. She never seemed to take time off. How she survived, I do not understand, as sometimes the Parade was still open at 4 a.m.

She altered the décor very little since the days of Jay Haselwood, so in consequence it retained much of the atmosphere he created. Eugenia Bankhead's (Tallulah's sister) black satin evening shoe, with its exceptionally high *diamanté* heel, still stood on a gilt wall bracket getting dustier and more tarnished every year. Lily had a feeling that to move it would bring bad luck, as Eugenia and Jay were like a brother and sister.

Jay was a great showman and, thanks to his magnetic personality, the Parade Bar in Tangier was as well known a name to Americans as the Ritz Bar is in Paris. He died at the early age of forty-eight. His heart could not stand the strain of the late hours and endless whiskies. Lily drank cups of tea and lived until 1980.

Mrs Selwyn, a rich Australian married to a retired purser from the P&O Lines, was a particularly unpleasant woman. She went by the unsuitable name of Twinkles. His name was Percy. When Sir Stafford Cripps, the Chancellor of the Exchequer in the Labour Government, announced that he would remunerate anyone who identified persons he knew were getting money out of England illegally, Twinkles bristled with excitement. A nice, harmless English couple, Mr and Mrs Hartley, were living here at the time.

He had a serious heart-disease and had been forbidden by his doctor to winter in England. It was obvious to all that they could not possibly be living the way they were on the pittance allowed them by the Treasury, but as Mr Hartley was a very sick man, people closed their eyes to this. Not so Twinkles, who set to work, in the name of patriotism, to prove their dishonesty. She succeeded and they were heavily fined. Twinkles got a golden handshake, and Mr Hartley died of shock.

A French woman, Françoise Vijnet, advertised in the local paper for a new maid. The maid duly arrived and Françoise asked her why she had left her last employer (who happened to have been Twinkles).

'They were robbers, madame.'

'In what way?' asked Françoise. 'And what proof have you of this?'

'Well, madame, all their bed-linen, towels, cloths, cups, saucers, plates, knives, forks and spoons were embossed with the initials "P&O".'

Percy was a timid, good man. He owned a parrot almost as old as himself, and which he loved. When he was very ill and knew that he had not much longer to live, he asked Twinkles, who detested the bird, to give it after his death to Mercedes Guitta, a friend and great animal lover. He also told Mercedes that Polly would be hers. A week or so after he died, Mercedes telephoned Twinkles and asked for the parrot. 'I've wrung its neck,' she replied, and rang off.

Twinkles got her just deserts. Without Percy, she was invited nowhere, and slowly she became mentally deranged. She lived alone, sacked the servants, had the water cut off, so that she never washed, used the apartment-house stairs as her lavatory, subsisted on scraps and stale leftovers from the bottom of half-empty tins. She was engrained with dirt, and when eventually the police broke into her flat, she was unconscious and was thus taken to the Italian Hospital, where the saintly nuns had literally to scrape off the dirt. She died alone, unloved and unregretted.

Nellie Likatcheff, German and married to a Russian, was an extraordinary woman. She was beautiful in a grotesque way. Tall and red-haired, she spoke English with a strong accent. Her clothes were remarkable in that nothing matched. Only once did I see her dressed correctly, and that was when she gave a reception in her large house soon after the war. All the guests were assembled in the great hall, but there was no sign of Nellie. At the height of the party she appeared at the top of the marble staircase, dressed entirely in black with a vast black satin bow pinned to the back of her hair. She held up her hand for silence and proclaimed, 'I am sorry I can't come down, but I am on the British Foreign Office's black list. Enjoy yourselves.' She then retired, not to appear again that evening.

She drove around Tangier in a black limousine, wearing either enormous bows in her hair or huge picture hats and ropes of pearls from her throat to her stomach. When she saw me in the street she would tell the chauffeur to stop. 'Come in, David, and have a chat.' I would get in, and there sat Nellie dressed properly only from the middle up. Below, she was in her petticoat and barefooted. I asked why she was always half dressed. She answered, 'As I never get out of the car, what is the use of dressing below window-level?'

Louise de Meuron was Swiss and was married against her will to a childhood friend named Tiger. She had two daughters but was not happy. Her mother was of an ancient family and a vast landowner, a true matriarch. She ruled the family with a rod of iron. They were all terrified of her.

One day Louise could bear it no longer and ran away. She arrived in Tangier almost penniless and went into hiding. Her mother and husband attempted to prove her insane to avoid a divorce. Tangier was an International Zone at that time, so Louise felt fairly safe, but she had not reckoned with her mother, who put Interpol on to finding her. Louise was warned just in time and fled across the border into Spanish Morocco, where she disappeared entirely for several months. The chase was given up finally, and Louise returned to Tangier.

After many years an arrangement was made and she obtained her divorce. Tiger married again, and Louise settled down here in an old Moorish house situated on a wild piece of land full of brambles and weeds. Little by little she created the most beautiful garden in Tangier, full of exotic and rare plants. Parrots and peacocks had complete freedom. She adored animals of any sort and would make a home for any stray creature she found.

She was full of life, making up for lost time spent incarcerated with her mother and Tiger in Switzerland. She always said she became *déclassée* because she had a Moroccan lover, which in the early days was considered impossible. Some nasty lady said to her, 'Madame de Meuron, you must be very rich.'

'Why do you think that, madame,' replied Louise.

'Because you have so many Moroccan lovers.'

'But madame, they are so cheap,' she answered.

Freddie Lumb was an Anglo-Indian colonel. He never smiled, and disapproved of everything and everybody. No one could resist teasing him, he was so pompous. His wife, Eva, was a delightful person – beautiful, cultivated and a first-rate gardener. As the colonel grew older he became senile, and when Eva went to his room, he thought she was the sergeant-major of his erstwhile regiment and would shout at her, 'Good God, man, what do you think you are doing here? Back to the barrack-room.'

Eve Chitenden was the local nurse in Tangier at the time and many old people were succoured by her until they died. One evening Eve was walking in the garden when Colonel Lumb rose from his bed, grabbed an old Mauser-Rigby rifle that was hanging on the wall and shot at her through the window. 'Got him!' he cried. He thought she was a tiger.

When he died his wife remained here until a few years ago, when she went back to England to enter a home for elderly gentlewomen. The owners are friends of hers, so she has the run of the garden, and I believe is happy. We miss her, not only for her company, but for the advice she gave us about gardening in this part of the world.

The English community has dwindled, not so much in numbers as in personalities. In the old days Tangier attracted individual people – people with character, eccentric, tragic people, wicked people, but seldom ordinary people. Now for the most part they are ordinary. I suppose it is the same the world over. There is no time for eccentricity because leisure has ceased to exist. Everyone is too busy merely trying to make ends meet.

Eve Chitenden was the only remaining eccentric. She never had enough money to live on, but nothing would persuade her to get rid of her dozen cats, several dogs and tame hens. She lived in one room; the hens lived in coops around the wall and all were let out one by one for exercise and conversation. Eve never grumbled, and I think she was helped by kind friends when she was in desperate straits.

Sonia and Narayan Kamalakar lived in a tent on the Marshan for several years. She was Russian, and her first husband was Prince Dragadze, by whom she had two sons and a daughter. Narayan, her second husband, was Indian, thin as a piece of brown paper, while she was as round as a pumpkin. They were both eccentrics, to say the least. Mystics and vegetarians, penniless and generous, they were forever seeing flying saucers long before such became the fashion. Sonia was bubbling with humour, and Narayan was intensely serious.

Sonia had a series of drinking glasses that were solid glass of different colours – red, white and whisky-coloured. When she invited people for drinks, those she liked were given proper drinks; the antipathetic were given the solid glasses. It was a silly joke but amusing in a way, until one lady took a gulp and chipped her tooth.

Sonia held court every Sunday at tea-time – tepid tea, stale cakes and scintillating conversation. Her daughter, Tamara, became a ballerina. She was petite and pretty, with a shock of flaming hair, and she would hand round the uneatable cakes, not walking but dancing on her points as though she were the star of Covent Garden.

Jane Bowles was a great friend of the family. One evening she gave a party and Sonia sat, a vast mountain of flesh, in the middle of the sofa. She didn't move the entire evening, not even to greet people as they arrived. The sofa was small, and there was nowhere else in Jane's little flat for people to sit down. I stayed on after the guests had left.

Jane said, 'You can move now, Sonia, thank you.'

Sonia heaved herself to her feet, to display a large hole burnt in the middle of the sofa. Jane had ordered her to stay positioned over it and on no account to move. Sonia had merely obeyed.

She died here and is buried in our English churchyard. Narayan was desolate and decided he would walk to Holland. On reaching his goal, he expired from fatigue and undernourishment.

Tamara is now a schoolteacher in Georgia USA and a writer.

Princess Nina Mdvani, Barbara Hutton's sister-in-law by her first husband, is an amusing brigand. She gets through life penniless, but stays at the best hotels and demands the treatment of royalty. She first married Adrian Conan Doyle, but divorced him and then fought a lawsuit to get the royalties from his father, the famous Conan Doyle. She travels with her jewellery, though I don't think there is much left now, and gives it on arrival to the hotel where she happens to be staying, as surety. She remains there till somehow the bill is paid by some pitying friend.

Nina is tall, not beautiful, and short-sighted, but she has immense charm. Her second husband was a minor American poet, Anthony Harwood. They also separated, but he came back to her to die.

Barbara, for many years, was the pitying friend who paid up for her, but it became too much and at last 'the worm turned'. She had had enough, as Nina would come every year to the Minzah Hotel, when Barbara was in residence at her Casbah house. Nina entertained lavishly, giving luncheons and dinners. After her departure, which was always unexpected, Barbara footed the bills.

I was fond of her, but I have not seen her for many years. I am told that she is in a poor way physically and mentally. I have no idea where she is now living, but I believe she haunts the lounges of Claridges and the Ritz at the pre-lunch cocktail hour, hoping to get a free meal.

Barbara Hutton, Lloyd Franklyn, Ira Belline and I toured Morocco for about a fortnight in two cars. Barbara was at her best, drinking only Coca Cola. We were received everywhere like royalty. Whenever we stopped, the local Caid called on us and arranged parties with dance orchestras and superb food.

Having covered hundreds of miles south of the Atlas, we arrived in Marrakesh where Ira knew a painter called Raymond Duan. Barbara wanted to buy some paintings of Morocco and Moroccans for the house at Boubana outside Tangier that she had given Lloyd. Ira took us to a semi-detached villa in the European part of the town. We were shown into the sitting-room where we sat on an upright settee in a line, like birds on a perch. The room was hideous beyond belief. While his French wife gave us coffee, Raymond proceeded to display one picture after another. Barbara disliked them all and kept whispering, 'Let's get out of here.'

At last Raymond produced a picture of what he imagined one of Barbara's parties in her house in Tangier to be like. Barbara was touched and, though she disliked the picture, bought it. We left thinking we would never see him again.

A year after this visit, Barbara started receiving the most romantic poems from Raymond. At first she had no idea who had written the poems, as they were anonymous. Always easily flattered, she became more and more intoxicated by the exquisite references to herself. A normal reaction of any woman, but particularly for Barbara, who had had a long series of unhappy marriages, but always believed that the current husband was deeply in love with her, when he was more interested in her money. I warned Barbara to be careful, and told her that the poems were written by Duan's brother. She was angry with me for shattering her dream, and as a result we didn't see each other for several years. By then Duan was her seventh husband and had become Prince Champassak.

It was especially wounding for Barbara, who was a great beauty as well as sweet and intelligent. She always managed to pick the wrong husbands. In all the years I knew Barbara, I had seldom seen her so happy as she was with Lloyd. I feel that if the painter had not interfered, Barbara would have had many more happy years with Lloyd.

We became friends again, but I saw little of her, as she had become a semi-invalid and came to Tangier rarely. Alas, she is now dead, and died, through the machinations of her business manager, practically a pauper.

Prince William of Gloucester, who was working in Nigeria, used to stop off on his way home to England and stay with me for a few days. He usually arrived in his private aircraft which he piloted himself. On one occasion he had done a job in Gibraltar and was coming over for a short holiday. As he wished to be incognito, he came not in his own aircraft but by Bland Line, which is now called Gibair. They unfortunately did not keep it to themselves, and the Governor of Tangier and the British Ambassador from Rabat were at the airport to meet him. I had no time to warn William to expect an official reception, so I asked the British Ambassador if, when the plane touched down, I could go ahead to do so.

Poor William, thinking he was an ordinary passenger, stepped out of the aircraft in an open-necked shirt and flannel trousers, and with unruly hair. He was so handsome that it didn't matter, but he was horrified. I said, 'Don't worry. Everyone will love you like that.' Before we could say more, a beautiful Moroccan girl came forward with an oversized bouquet of flowers. He accepted it gladly and charmingly, but, seeing the cameras about to click, I grabbed it from him just in time. Afterwards he said, 'Thank God you took the flowers. A bouquet of flowers for a man – that is something my father would not understand, being a military sort of chap!'

During one of Prince William's visits to me, Barbara Hutton was giving an exotic party in her palace in the Casbah. William and I and his ADC were invited to dinner before the dance. When we arrived on purpose a few minutes late, there was no sign of the hostess. The other guests were assembled punctually, as they had been told who the guest of honour was to be. I took William around and presented him to each. Champagne flowed, canapés of foie gras and caviare were handed round, and time passed quickly enough. Eventually Barbara, half an hour late, made her entrance. She looked unbelievably beautiful, ablaze with fabulous jewels. William had never met her and was completely taken aback by her lovely appearance. As was always the case with Barbara, when she wished to she could charm. She was at her best – gracious, smiling and every inch a princess. As she herself said, 'Darling, I ought to play the part well as I've been a princess three times!'

The party was a success, with moonlight on the terrace, belly-dancers in the courtyard, a Moorish orchestra on the roof and a dance band in the ballroom. By four o'clock we felt that it was time to leave. As we were saying goodbye, Barbara produced a beautiful caftan and presented it to William. Another one was given to his

ADC. Everyone had consumed a great deal of champagne and Barbara, on trying to make her reverence, could not quite do it. William was embarrassed and seized her hand.

'Wait a minute, sir,' said Barbara in her gentlest voice. 'Please let go of my hand. I am going to try again. See, I have made it,' she said, doing a deep curtsy to the ground. 'But if you don't mind, sir, I think I will stay where I am!' And so she did: on the floor!

When Barbara was 'on the wagon', she was amusing and intelligent. She would laugh at silly jokes, get fits of the giggles if you were in that mood, or talk seriously about life, politics, the latest books or plays if she sensed that was what you wanted. She was not only beautiful, but gentle and affectionate, so it was cruel of fate to make her an alcoholic. I have known people with whom somehow it didn't seem to matter whether they were alcoholic, but with Barbara it was unsuitable, for by nature she was clean, tidy, immaculately turned out and slightly disapproving. She also had perfect manners and great dignity. All these charming attributes disappeared when she drank. She slurred her words, the mascara ran in rivulets down her cheeks, the lower part of her face became smeared with lipstick, and she staggered about the room holding on to anybody or anything for support. During these alcoholic bouts, which sometimes lasted two weeks, she never slept, and her friends – or more aptly hangers on – were expected to remain with her round the clock. It was during these periods that she gave away so much of her jewellery to the surrounding vultures.

Another of her habits was to telephone people all through the night, sometimes three or four calls to the same person. She made very little sense, but it was no good hanging up because she would ring again, unaware that she had just talked to you. Sometimes these conversations would end in maudlin, loving words, at other times in furious abuse, but most frequently in floods of self-pitying tears. Poor Barbara. It was sad for those who loved her and knew her well, because in her case it certainly was not *in vino veritas*.

Barbara's parties were always beautifully staged, but to say they were always successful would be an exaggeration. If she was in a good and happy mood, Barbara was a perfect hostess. If she was tired or sad or had had too much to drink beforehand, her parties could be a disaster. On these occasions she would sometimes not appear the whole evening. Naturally this made people nervous. If she had sent a message saying, 'I am not well, but do enjoy yourselves and have a lovely time', all would have been fine, but she didn't, so we waited around, talking to each other, looking every other minute at the door through which she should appear. The orchestra played on in a dreary fashion, and there was a little desultory dancing, but when finally we realized that Barbara would not join us, the party died and, little by little, people drifted home.

Other parties were a great success, with Barbara at the top of her form: delicious food, champagne flowing, cabaret of belly-dancers, flamenco singers, Spanish dancers and Moroccan acrobats.

The house had several terraces, on one of which Barbara would receive her guests seated on a gilded throne surrounded by piles of coloured cushions made of Thai silk, and people were brought up to her as though she were a lady of royal birth. These people would sit at her feet on the lovely cushions and worship at the shrine! This sounds pretentious, but for Barbara it was pure theatre, for when she had had enough of the admiring sycophants, she would spring to her feet and dance the night away with all and sundry. She was irresistible because she was a creature of so many different moods. This is what made her such a fascinating character.

Barbara's house was situated in an overcrowded part of the Medina surrounded by small Moroccan houses. As the parties took place on the terraces, we were in full view of the outside world. The Moroccans enjoyed themselves just as much as the guests. They loved the lights, the music, the women's lovely dresses. They had the feeling that they were in some way just as much guests as we were, and remained enjoying themselves till the party ended.

These parties continued till dawn, with Barbara saying good-night to every guest, looking incredibly lovely with her emerald tiara still in place and jewels sparkling in the early morning dawn. As the performers left, she handed them each a present – the girls received an exquisite caftan and the men burnouses made of the finest wool. Her generosity knew no bounds.

One of Barbara's most controversial parties was when the invited guests were to come dressed as members of the opposite sex. This truly put the cat amongst the pigeons, as many of her friends were strait-laced: diplomats, bankers, respectable Moroccan business men, government officials. And since these were still the international days, every nationality was represented, as well as the Tangier élite. Also amongst the guests were hairdressers, cabaret artists and pianists from the current nightclubs. In fact, as the French said, 'Tout Tangier'. The evening was unforgettable, the effect bizarre, to say the least. Elderly ladies, middle-aged ladies, young ladies with beards and moustaches were dressed in dinner-jackets or business suits, while the men were in full *décolletée* evening dresses and wore blond wigs, black wigs, auburn wigs, their hairy arms and chests flowing over false bosoms, and their faces heavily made up, probably by their wives. The evening, after a difficult start, became hilarious. All shyness disappeared and people became almost abandoned, the most unlikely ones the most abandoned of all.

I shall never forget the end of the evening. Men's make-up was running down their cheeks, their eye-black so smudged they looked like giant pandas. Their wigs were askew, their bosoms slipping one high and one low. The women now had half a moustache or half a beard, and their hair plastered flat with grease began escaping from nets.

Of course Barbara knew it was an outrageous and daring idea but she had the courage to try it out. In contrast to the guests, she was exquisitely dressed as Robin Hood! Many people were unrecognizable, which added to the fun.

Barbara's small dinner parties were never much fun. It is difficult to explain why they were dull. Perhaps it was because she preferred either to be with one or two friends or to be surrounded by hundreds. We would get through dinner, which was always good, in a remarkably short time, soon after which Barbara would say good-night and retire upstairs, taking with her one of the guests – not for any ulterior purpose, as it could either be a man or a woman. After a few minutes classical music would waft down from the windows on to the patio where we were finishing our coffee. The records were always first-rate and sung by the best singers of that period.

Last year part of the life of Barbara Hutton was televised here. Mr Perski, a friend of mine, was the producer. He arrived with a large cast to shoot scenes in Tangier where she had spent so many happy years. Farrah Fawcett played the lead and resembled Barbara in an uncanny way. No one could have been more charming or elegant, and we spent much time together. Since Barbara had been a lifelong friend of mine, I thought I could help Farrah in a small way to understand her character. She listened attentively to what I had to say and asked me pertinent questions about Barbara's changing moods. For me, the result was wonderful. She portrayed Barbara exactly the way I hoped she would, and I trust the film will help to counteract the horrible biography which was written about her.

Before the company left, Farrah gave me a photograph of herself thanking me for, as she put it, 'Your endearing encouragement'. I was very touched.

I am also depicted in the film. The young man Nigel Le Galant who played me was also keen to make my acquaintance for much the same reason as Farrah Fawcett. He wanted to see what sort of person I was so that he could make the character as much as possible true to life. Of course I am many years older now than the age at which he portrayed me, but there was just enough resemblance to make it amusing for me. Mr Perski told me he had picked Nigel for that reason.

In the fancy-dress party scene, Mr Perski insisted that I should appear, looking I thought pretty silly in a flowing caftan and vast turban, out of which sprouted an ostrich feather. It was a fascinating, agreeable three weeks, particularly afterwards, as there were no fights and practically no flights of temperament.

In Tangier Barbara remains a legend to this day; the poor Moroccans had no feeling of resentment against her or her wealth. The local guides still proudly point out to tourists of every nationality, who have probably never even heard of her, 'You see there the Palace of the Woolworth heiress, Barbara Button!'

The last time she was in Tangier, a few years before she died, I received a large parcel. I untied the ribbon and continued to untie ribbon after ribbon as the package got smaller and smaller. Finally there lay a small round object wrapped in cotton wool, a golden egg. On the card was written: 'For darling David, from the goose that has laid so many golden eggs.'

When I emigrated to Morocco, Jamie Caffery came with me. He was the nephew of the American Ambassador in Paris and had lived in my house at Wilton for some years. Jamie's was a wasted life – he should have been a writer or an historian. He was a fount of knowledge and possessed a completely retentive memory. He had a deeply unhappy nature; he told me that he had never once woken up without turning his face to the wall and thinking, Oh God, another day. Inevitably he became an alcoholic. I did my best with all the devotion of which I was capable to reassure him and cure him of drink. The treatment had the opposite effect to what I intended. He could not bear my surveillance and left for Spain.

In Spain he created a niche for himself as a landscape gardener. Rich Americans and English flocked to the Costa del Sol. Jamie designed and subsequently tended their gardens, as most of them rarely spent more than a few months there during the season. Little by little drink got the better of him. People began complaining that he never turned up when expected, that he forgot the orders they had given before leaving. In the end, apart from a loyal few, they found someone more reliable.

The last time he came to stay with me, he told me that the doctors said that if he touched alcohol from now on he would die, as his liver could take no more. I was pleased to see him drinking only fruit juices and felt that perhaps he had at last been given a shock and would heed the warning.

He left for Spain two days later. The following day he died. I said to Mohamed, my servant, 'Poor Señor Jamie – how sad. He was doing what the doctors ordered, drinking only fruit juice.'

'Oh no,' said Mohamed. 'Each glass was three-quarters vodka, but he begged me not to tell you.'

His death ended a long chapter of my life. Now, at my advanced age, I realize what a fool I have always been. No one wants to be changed, let alone be cured of something he enjoys. There is a missionary side to my character which unfortunately makes it impossible for me to love anyone who, I think, does not need my help.

Bob Lebus, the younger son of the founder of the Lebus Furniture Company, had been an acquaintance of mine for many years before he bought a house in Tangier. He was a difficult character to understand. He was a perfectionist with a deep inferiority complex, which was unnecessary, as he was rich, kind and nice looking. It was impossible to be a real friend of his because he was always on the look-out for a snub, and consequently I had always to mind my Ps and Qs and think before I spoke. He was a social climber, but never really made the grade. He would climb five rings of the ladder, and then say or do something stupid and slip down three. This quality made him an unhappy man. His sister felt that if he had stayed with friends of his own world, he would have been a relaxed and contented person. For instance, if I said something which to him sounded snobbish, and he thought that I was patronizing him, he would reply, 'It's all very well for you, born at Wilton rather than in darkest Portman Square.'

'But Bob, Portman Square is a very good address. I don't see why you should be ashamed of it.'

The truth, his sister told me later, was that they were not born in Portman Square, and went there only when they were nine or ten years old. They were born a great deal less grand.

Olga Lynn, the singer, whom we all loved, was an alluring woman, but always in need of money. Bob used her as his climbing ladder, and Oggie was rewarded by trips abroad and substantial presents of money. She called Diana Cooper her carrot, because Oggie was always dangling Diana's name in front of Bob and then snatching it away at the last moment.

One evening Diana and I were driving in London and she said, 'I'm sick of being Oggie's carrot. I know she's having dinner with poor Bob Lebus at his flat in George Street. I'm going to call her bluff and gatecrash after our dinner.'

I dropped Diana at the flat and waited in the shadows while she rang the bell. The butler answered and Diana said, 'Is Mr Lebus in?'

'I'm afraid he's at dinner, madame. What name shall I say?'

'Lady Diana Cooper.'

'Oh yes, milady,' and he bustled off.

Hardly had Diana and I had time to exchange a look when Bob appeared, pink with excitement, his napkin still in his hand, begging her to come in and join them. Diana went in, and I slunk down the stairs.

Afterwards, Diana told me Oggie's face was as black as thunder

– and no wonder, since after all her golden carrot had been removed!

However, Diana was not the only carrot. There were many minor ones whom Oggie did introduce to Bob. They were mostly foreigners. For instance, if Oggie wanted to go to Venice in August, Bob would finance her, and in return she would take him to all the grand dinners and balls to which she had been invited. One winter he took her to New York. Diana wrote to Oggie saying: 'I hope you are doing your stuff by Bob.' Oggie answered: 'Little Bob is holding his own.'

I think Bob was happier here than anywhere else. Tangier is not grand, and there is nowhere to climb. He settled down to make many friends. He was, I know, more sure of himself. He could be very entertaining and gave enjoyable parties. One of his friends in England said, 'I can't understand why Bob is so happy in Tangier. After all, his ambition in life has been to meet the most important people in society, and they do not exist in Tangier.'

I answered, 'That is why he is happy. There is nowhere to climb to, except perhaps my cousin, Veronica Tennant, and myself, and he has got there, a remarkably short ladder though it is.'

Bob was Jewish but, strangely enough, hopeless about money. He once said, 'Isn't it odd that I have no business sense with all this rich blood coursing through my veins?'

He died in Madras and was cremated. There was no other way. And all his life he had a horror of fire.

Bob left his house to the Sherif and Sherifa of Ouezzane, who were his best Moroccan friends. The Sherif is the grandson of the well-known Englishwoman Emily Keene, who married the old Sherif in 1874. She became a great matriarchal figure in the Muslim world, though she herself always remained Christian. She once said to Jessie Green, 'My sons will not be much good, but you will see, if you are still alive, that my grandsons will all do well.' She was perfectly right. They all have important posts in the Administration of Morocco.

I remember once going to tea with the old Sherifa in her house on the Marshan, Juliet Duff took me and was very excited at the meeting. We went into a hall. The linoleum which covered the staircase was green with red swastikas. Her sitting-room might have been a lodging-house in England, with its overmantel covered with knick-knacks and the chimney-piece draped in red serge edged with a fringe of bobbles.

Juliet started talking away in a rather flustered, gushing manner. The Sherifa put up her hand and said, 'Lady Juliet, sit down, stop twittering, and tell me what you thought of Harold Nicolson's article in the *New Statesman* last week.'

Oggie Lynn was as round as a ball. She had fair hair, lovely skin, large but beady brown eyes, and was the smallest woman I have ever seen. In fact she was so short that on one occasion, when she was already on her feet, she was told to stand up during 'God Save the King'. She was an inch and a half shorter standing than sitting! Her voice was lovely. She had been trained by Jean de Reszke and it was a joy to listen to her when she sang to us after dinner. She was immensely greedy, hence her shape. She was also diabetic and would sneak into the dining-room and whip all the icing off a cake.

Her great friend, some people say her daughter, was Maud Nelson. She was Cecil Beaton's secretary. Once during the war Cecil had managed to get a beautiful fresh salmon as a present for his mother. When Mrs Beaton came round to collect this rare delicacy, it was nowhere to be found. Cecil was furious, then sent for Maud and said, 'Where's that salmon for my mother?' Maud burst into tears, dropped on her knees, and with her hands clasped together as though in prayer said, 'Forgive me, forgive me, but Oggie had to have it.'

When Oggie died, Maud took to drink and became totally bald. She had relations living in Portugal and some years ago came to visit friends here who owned a night-club called the Ranch Bar. She telephoned me and I invited her to lunch. I had asked other people to meet her to make it an occasion, as I hadn't seen her for years. She arrived but I didn't recognize her. No one had told me she was bald, and owing I suspected to a drink too many, she had omitted to put on her wig. Down the stairs came what I thought was a bald-headed old man with a few grey hairs sprouting unwillingly on his pate. As he was wearing trousers and a blazer, my reaction was not surprising.

'How do you do?' I said, and was about to say, 'I think you have come to the wrong house' when she spoke.

'David, darling, how lovely to see you!'

For a second I was speechless – then one, two, three, go! 'Maud, darling, how well you look. What fun to see you in Tangier! Do have a drink.'

I had no time to warn the guests. They, too, were amazed by her, but they behaved in a splendid way. Lunch was a success, and I shall never know whether poor Maud realized she had forgotten her wig.

David Edge, flamboyant, witty, crooked and entertaining, possessed great flair. He was a compulsive liar. Hardly a word of truth passed his lips. Everything was in his imagination. His palace in Luxor, his pavilion near Beirut, and several other castles in Spain were non-existent. As he got older, he became more exotic, wearing only caftans day and night, and always bedecking himself with second-rate jewellery.

I believe he started life studying to be a singer and eventually sang small parts in opera. He is supposed to have been 'picked up' by the Bishop of Hungary, who tried to get him a job at La Scala, Milan. On account of this, so the story goes, the bishop was defrocked and settled down with David Edge in the English countryside. After the death of the bishop, David inherited some money, and as the years passed he became a well-known figure in certain quarters of the art world. Always shady, he never quite made the grade, even in café society. The nearest approach to it came whilst he lived in a palazzo in Venice. The café society world will go anywhere there is a sniff of a party, and David Edge gave parties. Eventually he left Venice under something of a cloud and returned to London.

For many years I had heard stories about this mythical figure – some are better left untold – but I never met him until he came here and bought a tumbledown palace in the Casbah. This house was refurbished and filled to overflowing with *objets d'art* – some good, some bad, some fake, but flamboyant like himself. The house, like so many old Moorish houses, had no windows, but most of such houses have an open patio in the centre, on to which the rooms open. David Edge's patio was closed, with a small skylight in the roof. This was the only ray of daylight that filtered into this vast patio, which was crowded with objects of every description: tables, chairs, pictures, carpets on the walls, Chinese pots, plates, gongs and potted palms. In an alcove stood his canopied bed with hangings of tarnished gold and a jewel-encrusted bedspread. Most of the objects were covered with a layer of dust. The effect was theatrical, the atmosphere sinister.

David was knowledgeable and well informed about a great many things, if only he stuck to the truth. He was a good raconteur and could hold your attention for hours. At other times he was an impossible vulgarian, losing his temper and using the filthiest language. Everything about him was exaggerated – his speech, his gestures and his stories.

One evening at a party, he said, fingering his necklace, 'All my gold is twenty-eight carat.'

Gordon Sager, an American writer friend of mine, said, 'But David, I thought the best and purest gold was twenty-four carat.'

'Nonsense, my dear boy, twenty-eight.'

A drunken woman present piped up, 'Of course David is right. All my gold from Brazil is twenty-eight carat.'

On the surface, he put on a show of great opulence and unending resources. In fact he never knew where the next penny was coming from, and the last year of his life he was kept by a young Spaniard, Adolfo de Velasco, whom he had befriended and started in the antiques business. Adolfo has a shop in Tangier and a boutique in Marrakesh. He was the first to promote the caftan for European women and alter them just enough to suit the European way of life without detracting from the original Moroccan design. Adolfo is a friend of mine, and though he has not got the knowledge that David Edge possessed, in my opinion he has a great deal more taste. He is a man of greater charm and a thorough 'life enchanter'. Hard-working and ambitious, he has succeeded in making a name for himself in the international world of couturiers. He is an excellent public relations man, and has a particular flair for publicity, which has been half the battle for him in making himself known in the art and fashion world. He has astuteness as to what people want, and will go to London and come back with just the objects people here or in Marrakesh wish to buy. He is generous to a fault and totally unmischievous. He is devoted to his friends and will go to any length to defend them if he hears them criticized. I remember one evening at the Parade Bar when David Edge launched a vitriolic attack on Ira Belline. Naturally I retaliated, helped by Adolfo, who

1 The author's mother, the Countess of
Pembroke, in her role as Commandant
of the hospital at Wilton House during
the First World War.

2 The author's parents walking under
the famous cedar trees in the grounds of
Wilton House, 1939.

3 Sir Cecil Beaton in Tangier, *c.* 1983.

4 A luncheon picnic at Ashcombe, Wiltshire, the home of Cecil Beaton. Left to right: the author, Lady Bridget Parsons, Lady Gage, Lady Caroline Paget, Teresa Youngman, Tilly Losch, Tony Herbert (the author's younger brother), Mrs Shereen Smith and Cecil Beaton.

5 Lady 'Dandy' Paget, the author's maternal grandmother.

With so many good wishes for Christmas & the New Year - & all my thanks for those very attractive slippers.

Marina

6 Christmas card sent to the author from Princess Marina, Duchess of Kent, showing a portrait by the Princess of her daughter, Princess Alexandra.

7 Amateur play produced by Lady Harris. Left to right: Lady Colefax, the author, John Betjeman, Cecil Beaton and Osbert Lancaster.

8 Party at the house of Peter Owen to mark the publication of the author's book *Second Son*. Left to right: Lady Diana Cooper, Sir Cecil Beaton, the author.

9 The author with Barbara Hutton at a party at her house in Tangier.

also was one of Ira's many admirers. Nothing would stop this tirade, so I left the table. Adolfo rose and said to the others present. 'I think we will join David Herbert in the other room.' Mr Edge was left shouting abuse to himself.

I had never invited Mr Edge to my house and never intended to, but as the years rolled by he became a very sick man. He was lonely and sad. I was told that he longed to see my home, so I swallowed my pride and invited him to dinner. I asked the few friends he had left and one or two new acquaintances. The dinner turned out to be a success, as he was on his best behaviour, and the evening passed pleasantly.

Three weeks later he was dead. The ramifications of his will were countless. He had lived here twenty years and, by surreptitious means, somehow managed to remain a tourist. The house and effects were sealed by order of the Tangier tribunal. Adolfo was left nothing, not even (as he himself says), 'a dirty word'.

Adolfo still has his shop here and his boutique in Marrakesh. He is one of the best-known Europeans in Morocco and a friend of the royal family. He travels all over the world showing his collections of beautiful embroidered caftans. Last year he went to Japan, where he had a great success. This is much appreciated by the authorities here, as it is good propaganda for their exports.

The Hubrechts – Daan and Peggy – were fairly recent additions to Tangier. He was Dutch, she Canadian, brought up in England. Daan, who died several years ago, was a handsome, kind and thoroughly Christian man, though not a professing one. He and his family lost a large fortune when independence came to the Dutch East Indies. This was entirely the fault of Daan's father who, against all the advice of the family, refused to sell out at the opportune moment. Daan was an ambassador – good-looking, not particularly clever, but a splendid actor, and proved a success in his diplomatic career. His wife was an adorable woman; a painter, completely honest and Bohemian.

Peggy was a complex character. She loved Daan and suffered acutely during the last cruel years of his life. He died of cancer; her younger brother a few years before had undergone an operation for the same disease. This brother recovered but can speak only in a whisper. A year later her elder brother died also from cancer, so that in two years she lost two of the three most important people in her life. Peggy had enormous courage and came through these tragedies with flying colours. She gave the impression of being a domineering, efficient, rather hard woman, whereas in reality she was ultra-feminine and deeply sensitive.

Peggy's one great fault, as I often told her, was that she possessed no censor cells. Everything she said came tumbling out without her considering the effect it might have, and this unhappily led to a lot of misunderstandings. She rarely got a name right or a story quite correct; and she had the reputation of being mischievous, which she was not. I once said, 'Peggy, do think before you speak.' She answered, 'How can I? I don't know what I'm going to say till I've said it.'

This reminds me of another little story. During a lunch given by a mutual friend, Bob Lebus was there, so was Peggy, whom he did not like. As Bob was speaking about a delightful time he had spent in Florence and how he had met a wonderful antique dealer, Peggy, who had also lived in Florence, was trying to join in the conversation. She was rudely interrupted by Bob, who said, 'You could not possibly have met this man!'

'Oh, really!' said Peggy, 'This "wonderful man" happened to be my first husband!'

Peggy had many loyal friends from all parts of the world, for she was kind, understanding and amusing. Her greatest friend here was Patricia Erzini, a beautiful young Englishwoman who married a Moroccan some twenty years ago. They were at Cambridge University during the same period, but they had never met until one day Patricia, who is an excellent harpist, was struggling with her vast musical instrument, attempting to put it on the train for London. Abdelkader Erzini saw this ravishing girl and went to her assistance, probably saying, 'May I assist you with your harp?' Anyway, it was love at first sight – they have five children and are as happy as they were the day they met at Cambridge railway station.

This disproves completely that East is East and West is West. It is one of several happy marriages that I know of between European women and Moroccan men.

PART THREE

Tangier is a sophisticated village, and its quality of sophistication gives it a charm which is unique. However, this charm and the easy-going life that we lead here would be monotonous without visitors from other places. It often happens that the telephone rings just as I am thinking how nice it would be to see a new face. I pick up the receiver and an unknown voice says, 'Hello. Is that David Herbert?'

'Speaking.'

'You don't know me, but a mutual friend told us to get in touch with you. Perhaps you could come and have a drink with my wife and me this evening at the Minzah Hotel and tell us where to go and what to see on our trip down south.'

'Thank you so much. I should be delighted, and I hope if you are still here tomorrow you will both lunch or dine with me.'

Sometimes these chance encounters develop into new friendships; at other times they turn out to be a little tedious. Even so, they add variety to life here.

Old friends and members of my family, who come and stay with me for a week or two, are not in that category. Usually when they come and stay for a period of time, we go together on trips to the south of Morocco, over the Atlas Mountains as far as the Sahara Desert. This part of my book is devoted to all my visitors and my family.

I was astonished, when the post arrived one morning, to receive a letter from my mother suggesting that I should go to Gibraltar and stay with her for a week; then perhaps she would come over and spend a week with me.

My mother visited me in Morocco only once. She had always resented my leaving England, and by then she was already an old lady, though still beautiful and still indomitable. She brought with her Violet Wyndham, as a companion. Violet was not one of the world's beauties – in fact, she was nicknamed 'Auntie Nose' – but she was amusing and witty and had written several excellent books. My mother treated her as a lady-in-waiting, which Violet did not like, so although my mother was enjoying herself, Violet was restless and obviously anxious to return home. Every other day she would bring up in conversation the departure times of flights to London and of boats to Gibraltar, until my mother was so irritated she practically told her to shut up. Violet burst into tears. My mother said, 'Stop behaving like a teenage girl – you are well over seventy. Go upstairs, dry your eyes, and don't come down until you've got control of yourself.' Violet came down to dinner, dry eyed but resentful.

The next morning my mother said to me, 'Was I awful to Violet last evening?'

I said, 'Yes, you were.'

'Well,' said my mother, 'take me into the town, and I'll buy her a little cedarwood box in which to keep her costume jewellery. That will cheer her up.'

The visit passed off better than I had expected. They left for Gibraltar and there Violet came into her own. She loved young men and had a splendid time with the Governor of Gibraltar's ADCs. My mother scoffed at this – ADCs were small fry to her.

In truth, my mother resembled an eighteenth-century aristocrat. I am sure she would have been the first to go to the guillotine, and would have gone with great dignity and courage, pitying the poor wretches who were about to behead her. Towards the end of her life she mellowed, but only up to a point. She could still be imperious and stubborn, having been accustomed to living in style and controlling Wilton and all its dependants. Being reduced to a London flat with a couple, it was hard for her to readjust herself. Everything had to be 'just so'. Couple after couple came and went, and my sister was driven almost demented searching for suitable replacements. Eventually she found the ideal pair, old-fashioned and in their seventies. They understood my mother, having been in domestic service all their lives. Apart from that, they had worked for the same sort of people as she was. He was an ex-soldier and had been batman to a friend of my father at the beginning of this century. They stayed with her until she died. It was rather a case of Queen Victoria and John Brown where he was concerned. When my mother became impossible and ticked him off, he would answer her back. One day after a battle between them, she said, 'The trouble with you is you are just a rough old soldier.' He replied, 'The trouble with you is that you are just a tough old countess.'

My mother died in her flat in London after a short illness. She was rising ninety. I arrived from Morocco just in time; she knew me and held my hand very firmly for a few minutes. She was semi-conscious and eventually died with my sister and me beside her. She looked incredibly beautiful, like a recumbent statue. Patricia and I said a silent prayer and went into the sitting-room.

'What prayer did you say?' I asked.

'The Lord's Prayer,' said Patricia.

'So did I,' I said.

'How unoriginal Mama must think us,' she replied.

My mother wished to be cremated, so arrangements were made with the crematorium at Golders Green. My sister and I were the only two to attend this sad and unreal ceremony with piped organ music and the coffin disappearing through a hatch, when the priest at the appropriate moment pressed the electric button. The episode lasted about ten minutes and, as we left, we were handed Mama's wedding-ring, which I have worn ever since on my little finger. We asked how long it would take to deliver the ashes to the flat. We wished this to be done as soon as possible, as we were to motor to Wilton where there was to be a short service in the private chapel and the following day a public service in the parish church. They said, 4.40 p.m. at the earliest.

Patricia and I went back to the flat; there were constant interruptions. The doorbell never ceased ringing with the delivery of flowers and fruit and the usual things sent to an invalid. Mama's death had not yet been published in the papers. At about 2.30 p.m. a small parcel arrived, delivered by a smart young man. 'Oh,' I said, 'is this for Lady Pembroke? I am afraid it is too late', and was about to tell him to take it back to the sender when apologetically he said, 'I am afraid, sir, this *is* Lady Pembroke.' They had brought the ashes two hours earlier than expected.

I walked into the sitting-room and before I could open my mouth, Patricia said, 'Oh dear, more chocolates for poor Mama.'

'No,' I said, 'It *is* Mama.'

We both laughed hysterically. My mother would have loved the joke and it broke the strain for us.

We arrived at Wilton about half-past six, and the little urn containing my mother's ashes was placed in the chapel where the Vicar of Wilton conducted a short service. For those left behind, I think that cremation is less harrowing than the ordinary burial service. It is impossible to imagine that a small urn contains the loved one who has died, whereas when a coffin is lowered into the earth it is heart-breaking. I shall certainly be cremated when I die, but I shall have to die outside Morocco, as there is no crematorium in this country.

The Wilton church was built in the Italian style by my Russian great-great-grandmother, and though it is too large for the size of the town, it is beautiful in its way. It is of golden grey stone, and has a high campanile which creates a strange effect in an old Wiltshire town. The altar faces north, as by religion the Russian Lady Pembroke was Orthodox. There was not an empty seat at the service for my mother, the church being crowded with people from all walks of life. The Mayor and Corporation were much in evidence in their robes, as my mother had been elected Mayor of Wilton three times during her fifty-two years as chatelaine of Wilton House, the home of the Herberts for over four hundred years. She had been respected and admired for all the public work she had done; and although she frightened some people with her directness, one and all admitted her sense of justice and dedication to whatever job she took on, and the efficiency with which she tackled any problem put before her.

After the service we drove to the family burial ground, which is situated in a dell in the Park. This dell is surrounded on three sides by a wood. The dell itself is planted with syringa and lilacs; an old barn built of black and white timber serves as a chapel. It is unlike a cemetery and has an atmosphere of complete peace. With the doves and pigeons cooing in the trees, pheasants calling in the wood, and smaller birds singing and twittering among the flowering shrubs, it is as near-perfect a resting-place as you could ever find. For generations the Pembroke family were buried in the old churchyard, which existed before the Italianate church was built. It was my mother's idea to create this haven for us among such lovely natural surroundings. Very few of us are buried there as yet: my mother and father, my two brothers, Sidney and Anthony, my cousins, Michael and Sydney Herbert, my uncle, Geordie Herbert, and Juliet Duff, whose famous mother, Lady Ripon, was born a Herbert. So there is plenty of room for me, and indeed for many future Herberts.

My grandmother on my mother's side was the daughter of Lord Combermere. She married Lord Alexander Paget, younger brother of the Marquess of Anglesey. He was a selfish individual and neglected her abominably. While he was visiting all the great houses of England and Scotland, where he was much in demand as he was a great shot, Granny was struggling to bring up four children on a very small allowance – so small that she decided to take the children to live in Paris where life was much cheaper. My mother told me that they were so badly off that until they were eleven or twelve they all wore sand-shoes, as leather shoes were too expensive. Granny loved three of her children, but she never really liked my mother. She found her too bossy; but my mother, strangely, adored her.

Lady 'Dandy', as she was called, was an eccentric. She was the first woman to have shingled hair; she dressed like an artist from the Quartier Latin – with lace jabots, velvet jackets with silk braid around the cuffs and lapels, full skirts of coloured tweed, black shoes with silver buckles, and a wide, floppy felt hat. A cigarette in a paper holder was seldom out of her mouth. She never smoked more than a puff or two, then removed the cigarette and put it back in her case. She was constantly offering one to people, who were startled at being confronted with a case full of stubs.

She had a faithful maid, Rosa, who was a religious maniac. She was always trying to inspire my grandmother by singing hymns outside her sitting-room door, accompanying herself on a battered guitar. One afternoon I was sitting with Granny when Rosa began 'Lead Kindly Light'. Granny whispered, 'Tiptoe across the room and fling open the door.' This I did and, as the door opened, a book whistled past my ear and landed with a thump on Rosa's chest.

During the General Strike in May 1926 Granny was to be seen at Hyde Park Corner driving a coach and four to Hammersmith as public transport, with Rosa on the box, and an elderly lady from Cheshire, Queenie Garnet, holding the horses' heads. Granny's great joke was, as soon as Queenie let go of the horses' heads, to whip up the animals so that the poor lady hardly had time to jump on to the steps of the coach as it galloped past her. All these ladies were over seventy.

My grandmother's poverty ended suddenly when the Marquess of Anglesey died. In reality, he was the illegitimate son of Coquelin, the French actor, and Lady Anglesey. He was a cretin and when playing ping-pong he wore suits designed by himself, embroidered with real jewels. He wrote plays and acted in them; he always played the female lead, and they were performed in the chapel. At these performances, which were frequent, there was inevitably a certain little man in the front row who applauded louder than anyone else. He had a small jewellers' shop in Bangor, the Welsh town across the Menai Strait from Anglesey. 'Ux', as the Marquess was called, visited the shop often and bought almost everything in it!

When my uncle Charles succeeded to the title, the estates Beaudesart in Staffordshire and Plas Newydd in Anglesey, and a vast fortune, my grandfather was dead. This wealth went to my grandmother's head. Naturally, after years of being very poor and bringing up four children on a pittance, she let herself go and became extravagant. She ordered horses and carriages, bought a large house in St John's Wood and a place for herself in the country. In fact, she had a wonderful time.

Her eldest daughter, my aunt Frid, married Lord Ingestre, son and heir to the Earl of Shrewsbury. Charlie married the beautiful Lady Marjorie Manners, sister of Lady Diana Cooper and daughter of the Duke of Rutland, and my mother married my father; so she justly felt that she had not done too badly in the rearing of her family. The only fly in the ointment was my uncle Victor, the adored youngest son. He was no good, and all through his life my uncle Charlie paid thousands of pounds in debts that Uncle Victor had incurred. He married the musical comedy actress, Olive May. We all loved her, but he treated her shamefully. Later she divorced him and married Lord Drogheda, the father of my friend Garrett.

Granny had a stroke while staying in Paris. The faithful Rosa was still with her. She telephoned my mother, who drove to Southampton at a moment's notice, took the night boat and arrived in Paris the next morning. The rest of the family took their time. When she arrived, Granny was unconscious. My mother, whose name was Bee, sat by her bedside for hours. She was tall and beautiful, and, as I have said, the least loved of the four children. Suddenly Granny regained consciousness, looked at my mother, and in a clear voice with a twinkle in her eyes said, 'It's long-legged Bee. It would be.' She then died – the rest of the family were too late.

My father was a soldier when my mother first married him. She understood and liked the life that being a soldier's wife entailed. She had many admirers, chiefly famous generals in the First World War, when Wilton was a hospital and she was the commandant. During the Second World War Wilton was Southern Command Headquarters, and a series of commanders-in-chief stayed there during their terms of office. My mother ruled Southern Command with a rod of iron. She insisted on a weekly inspection to see that there was no damage being done to the house. It might have been the Supreme Commander of the Allied Forces who was paying a visit, not just Lady Pembroke, mistress of the house. Generals, colonels, majors, captains were all as nervous as kittens on my mother's arrival each Monday morning. She was quite right, as certainly the damage would have been double if she had not insisted on these inspections.

There is a beautiful eighteenth-century temple, designed by Chambers, situated at Wilton in a wood on a hill in the Park overlooking the river, as well as the Palladian bridge and the Inigo Jones façade of the house. One day my mother found that the soldiers had been carving their initials on the graceful stone columns. She was furious and sent for the commandant. She made him walk with her up to the temple and said, 'Look what damage your soldiers have done to this beautiful piece of architecture. You have no discipline over them. It is disgraceful.'

The poor flustered man said, 'Perhaps it was the gale last week that has done the damage, Lady Pembroke.'

My mother drew herself up to her full height and said, 'Perhaps, Colonel, you are most fortunate than I am, in that you have witnessed gales carving initials deep into eighteenth-century stone columns. Have your men up here by two o'clock, erase the initials, and tidy up the place generally – and do not let this sort of thing occur again.'

Wilton is a dream of beauty in the spring with great clumps of daffodils, jonquils and narcissi under the huge trees and along the river-bank. My mother had planted these with loving care during her years of living at Wilton, and she guarded them fiercely. During the war they were picked, not indiscrimately, but carefully, so as not to spoil the effect, and sent to the hospitals and offices where the top brass worked. My mother was permanently at war with military females working there, for however much she attempted to stop the ATS and WAAF drivers from picking them, it became a losing battle. Once when I was home on leave walking with her in the garden, she caught a young woman grabbing at the flowers, pulling up the bulbs at the same time.

'How dare you steal my flowers!' said my mother.

'I've only taken a dozen,' the woman replied defensively.

'One or a dozen, it is the same thing. You are stealing – I shall see that you are reprimanded. Drop those flowers at once!'

My sister Patricia, Mary and David Crawford and I went for a trip over the Middle Atlas to Erfoud, a town in an oasis of palms, some nine miles from Rissani, the cradle of the Alaouite dynasty. There is very little of interest in Erfoud itself, but the hotel built to resemble a casbah is comfortable, and the setting a dream of beauty.

The first morning after our arrival we set out for Merzuga, an oasis in the desert forty miles away. The drive is startling; the desert slag is black. The roads are only tracks, which seem endless until suddenly you see hills of shocking-pink sand rising out of the black desert. The effect is amazing. At the end of this range of dunes you come to the town of Merzuga beside a great lake surrounded by desert wild flowers and inhabited by flamingos. The sense of unearthly peace we felt as we stood looking at this magical place was suddenly shattered by a strident, angry voice shouting in French. We approached to listen to this tirade, which was directed at a poor fourteen-year-old guide. The man was saying he was one of the best-known botanists in Belgium, and why couldn't this boy tell him the name of a certain desert flower.

Our guide, a little older, became angry and went over to the assistance of the boy, who by this time was in tears. The Belgian continued rebuking him. Our guide shouted, 'If you are such a well-known botanist, why don't you know the name of this flower?' The Belgian exploded with anger. We thought that there would be a fight, so we begged our guide to leave them. He said something in Arabic to the boy, who just walked away with our guide and left the botanist spluttering with frustrated fury whilst his timorous, mousy wife tried unsuccessfully to placate him.

Our guide could not get this encounter out of his mind. He went on and on about it. Finally he said, 'Of course, there are flowers without names in this part of the world. For instance, the other day I broke a stone with a hammer and inside was a flower. It couldn't have a name, could it?'

'Yes,' said Mary Crawford, 'Fossil.'

On our way back to Erfoud from Merzuga we passed a black Bedouin tent. The Bedouins beckoned us to come inside. It was large and divided in two by a wall of multicoloured cushions. There were carpets on the floor, mattresses to recline on, and small, circular cedarwood tables from which to eat. We were given hot, home-made bread with goat's cheese and honey, and glasses of mint tea. We sat in the men's side of the tent.

After our meal Mary and Patricia were taken to the women's quarters on the other side of the cushioned wall. When they returned, a good-looking young man asked our guide to inquire of Patricia if she knew anything about illness. He explained that he had had a sore throat for a very long time and had been burning the skin around his Adam's apple with a piece of hot iron. He showed us the scars.

Patricia declared, 'He has got quinsy and should go to hospital for treatment.'

'Oh,' said the boy, 'I've been there and they gave me all this.' He produced a box of injections and a bottle of pills.

'But', replied Patricia, 'you've only used two of the injections and the bottle of pills is hardly touched.'

'I know,' said the boy. 'They told me to have an injection twice a week and two pills each day, but I thought they would last longer if I took them just occasionally.'

'How long have you had them?' asked Patricia.

'It was the last time we came here from the Sahara – about six months, I think.'

Every time I fed my large blue macaw (which, alas, is now dead), I would remember his arrival from Rio, first class by air. He was sent as a present by Patricia Ellis, private secretary to our Ambassador, who since married and is now an ambassadress herself. Patricia, the tall, lovely daughter of Julie and Toby, was born in Tangier. Fortunately, as her father was not always as agreeable as he might have been, she took after her mother, an enchanting person, who died of some tropical disease shortly after I came to Tangier. Patricia and I became great friends.

One early spring, Patricia, Jamie Caffery and I drove to Marrakesh to join Diana Cooper and Iris Tree. They had been lent a house in the medina. We arrived in heavy rain to find Diana lying in a damp bed with a high temperature and a ferocious cough. Iris, as always vague, but irresistible, was not made to cope with illness; she was trusting to luck that Diana would recover without medical attention. Patricia, seeing how seriously ill Diana was, fetched a doctor who dosed her with antibiotics. She was forced against her will to stay in bed for several days. She recovered slowly, and we made plans for the trip ahead.

El Glaoui, the Pasha of Marrakesh, arranged our trip. At that time Diana was still British Ambassadress in Paris, and the Pasha all-powerful in the protectorate. According to our schedule, on the first day we were to lunch with Brahim, the eldest of his sons and Pasha of Telouet. He lived in a fairy-tale palace high up in the Atlas Mountains on the road to Ouarzazate.

We left Marrakesh early, and after a three-hour drive in the snow-covered mountains we turned off the main road and slithered down a frozen track for another hour or so until we came to a bridge at the bottom of the valley. Having crossed this, we started to climb again. The road was only just passable and the going slow and difficult. Suddenly, high above us, we had our first glimpse of this palace in the sky, its green-tiled roofs shimmering in the brilliant sun. They had obviously been swept by slaves, as it was the only splash of colour in that white world. As we drew near, the gates of the Casbah were opened, and we drove through several enormous courtyards, with frozen fountains, tubs of orange trees carefully protected with straw, and white peacocks strutting proudly. The cold was piercing.

Arriving at the front door, we were received by the major-domo, wearing flowing white robes and the traditional turban. We were then shown into a vast room of incredible beauty, with painted red-coloured tiles. There was no form of heating, and as the sun never penetrated the small, slitlike windows, it was colder inside than out.

We sat down and waited, while an endless stream of beautifully dressed girls offered us almond milk, mint tea, orange-juice, olives, nuts and delicious little meat and chicken pastries. Delicious, yes, but cold comfort. Luckily Jamie had a flask of whisky, and all took surreptitious nips from it and began to thaw. After what seemed hours, a fabulous meal was carried in – course after course of exotic Moroccan dishes borne on brass trays. Still no drink, and still no Brahim.

Brahim never arrived, so eventually we skidded down the mountain road and were climbing up the other side when we saw a cavalcade of horses coming towards us. The chauffeur stopped. 'It's the Pasha,' he said. Brahim was full of apologies. Apparently there had been some trouble in a neighbouring village, and he had been summoned by the headman to quell a minor revolution.

We drove on, and it was after dark by the time we got to Ouarzazate. There we received a truly royal welcome. The gates were flung open as we approached and a guard of honour lined up to greet Diana. There must have been scouts outside watching for our arrival, otherwise the timing could not have been so perfect. The second Glaoui son was on the steps to meet us, and we were shown into a small and lovely room, where we were offered whisky and soda, dry martinis – anything we asked for. The secretary then accompanied us to the hotel, where we were received with equal pomp. We rested, bathed and changed for dinner.

About nine o'clock the Pasha and his entourage fetched us and took us to the palace. As we entered the front courtyard, soldiers in uniforms presented arms. In the second courtyard there were about five hundred women dressed in shimmering gauze party clothes of every conceivable colour, bedecked with all the jewels they owned. An orchestra on a raised dais struck up, and the women danced themselves into a frenzy. Diana was so caught up in it all that she joined the women dancing. We were then given a banquet in one of the reception-rooms of the palace, whilst outside the party went on. After dinner we again took part in the revels and were taken home at three o'clock in the morning. It had been a long but marvellous day.

Four years ago Diana died at the age of ninety-three, still beautiful but bedridden: she longed for death and told me that every night, when saying her prayers, she ended with the words, 'Please, dear God, take me. Why the hell have you forgotten me?' I suggested one evening that she should change her tune and end by saying, 'Please, dear God, let me live for ever and ever.' Next morning the telephone rang. It was Diana. 'No good – still here, blast him.'

At moments she was in pain, and the doctor refused to give her morphine. She told me that one day she suddenly remembered Enid Bagnold, author of *The Chalk Garden, National Velvet* and many other books, giving her some boxes of the stuff just before she died. 'Wanda,' she cried to her devoted maid, 'get a chair and climb up to that cupboard above the bookshelves, and there you will find some small square boxes. Please bring them to me.' She opened one of them and, to her dismay, found written on the label: *No use after three years.* Enid had been dead for ten!

Diana had a little chihuahua which she called Doggie. She loved him; nobody else did. She took him everywhere, to theatres, cinemas, restaurants, snuggled in her fur muff. Some restaurants grew to be fond of him because they loved Diana, and he was allowed to peep out of his hiding-place and swallow a morsel of chicken.

Diana was a fearless, erratic and thoroughly bad driver; she broke every possible rule of the road. It was a nightmare to be driven by her in London. The older she got, the more dashing her driving became and, as for parking, that was no problem for Diana. She would park anywhere her fancy took her: on a zebra crossing, on a street-corner on double yellow lines, on the wrong side of the road. It made no difference to her. Having stopped on one of these delectable places, she would take out of her bag a piece of paper on which she had scrawled *Old cripple trying to get a bite. Have mercy,* and stuck it under the windscreen wiper. Nine times out of ten she got away with it. Once, after lunching together in a restaurant in Pimlico, we went out to the car to find that the warden had written at the bottom of Diana's note: 'Hope you had a good meal, Dearie. Good Luck.'

My aunt Bridget was married to my mother's youngest brother, Lord Victor Paget. After they were divorced, she never remarried. Bridget was a remarkably attractive woman without being a beauty – straight black hair, a rather long face, magnolia skin, pearly teeth and a superb figure. Her many admirers included the Prince of Wales. 'No one wanted to marry me, darling. I gave in too quickly. For instance, the Duke of Westminster proposed to me on a Tuesday. I went to bed with him that night and never saw him again.'

During the year the Prince of Wales became King, Bridget was asked to Sandringham, with Mrs Simpson as hostess. Bridget never had any money and couldn't afford a personal maid, so my mother lent her Miss Baker, who had been with her many years and was extremely grand and an ardent Roman Catholic convert. After the visit my mother asked her if she had enjoyed herself.

'I certainly did not, milady.'

'Why not, Baker?'

'Well, there we were two duchesses in the house, three countesses, Lady Victor and several other titled ladies – and would you believe it, milady, at meals in the steward's room That Woman's maid went in ahead of us!'

Bridget's chief criticism of Mrs Simpson was that she called the Prince of Wales David in public. 'How dare she! But of course she doesn't know you must either call him "Sir" or "Darling".'

This reminds me of the time the Duchess of Windsor and I were stuck on each side of the revolving door of the Ritz in the Place Vendôme. It took nearly an hour for the engineer to release us. It was embarrassing for both of us, as my family had sided with George VI and Queen Elizabeth – my sister having been her lady-in-waiting since she became Queen. (My brother and sister-in-law had been in-waiting to the Duke and Duchess of Kent.) Eventually the door partition was removed, and I must say the Duchess was splendid. 'Well, David,' she said, 'I suppose this is when we'd better say re-"how do you do".'

During this period the Duff Coopers were at the British Embassy in Paris. They gave an evening party at which the Windsors were to be present. The Duchess had not been created a royal highness and the conversation at every lunch and dinner for days before was whether the women should curtsy to her or not. Some said they would do so, others said they wouldn't. Lady Mendl, the veteran American-born interior decorator married to Sir Charles Mendl, summed up the situation by saying, 'Well, my dears, take my advice and stand with your back flat against the wall – then you *can't* curtsy.' Many took her advice.

Apart from a lapse with playboy Jimmy Donahue (Barbara Hutton's cousin), Wallis was a good wife to the Duke, however much she may be criticized.

I remember one amusing visit at Portofino. It was on Daisy Fellowes's yacht (her mother was a Singer Sewing-Machine and her father the Duc D'Ecosse). Daisy said, 'I really must ask the Windsors. I don't want to, but it seems so rude not to – poor things, shut up in a hotel.' Daisy had a streak of wickedness – she was determined that the party should be a failure. The guests included such well-known people as Ronald Colman and his wife, Benita Hume, Rex Harrison and Lilli Palmer, and of course Jimmy Donahue. She told everyone to dress in evening clothes except Jimmy, who arrived in beach attire. The Duchess was much annoyed and drew herself up saying, 'Really, Jimmy, you might have taken the trouble to change.'

'Oh,' replied Jimmy, 'so you don't like the way I dress, Wallis? OK, to hell with you.' And he dived over the side of the yacht into the filthy, stinking harbour.

Daisy enjoyed her evening immensely.

At another party given for the Windsors by Barbara Hutton at the Ritz in Paris, the Duke at the last minute was unable to come. However, the Duchess was the guest of honour and when dinner was announced the head-waiter went up to her and said, 'Votre Altesse est servie.' Then he went over and said the same thing to Barbara. I was talking to an American woman, Eleanor Loder, who had known the Duchess for many years. 'What's keeping Wallis?' she asked. 'Why isn't she getting up? Poor Barbara's standing waiting for her to go into the dining-room. God, will she ever learn?' With that she got up, went to the Duchess and said, 'Come on, Wallis, off your hunkers.'

For entertainment after dinner, Susie Solidor, the great French *diseuse* of that period, recited classical poetry. One particularly famous verse called 'Ouvré' drew a shocked expression from the Duchess. She sat stony-faced, behaving as she imagined a royal lady would behave. Again, Eleanor couldn't stand it and snapped, 'Wallis, take the surly expression off your face. That poem is a classic, not a dirty story!'

Even as far back as the Duke's death in 1972, the Duchess's mind wandered. When she came to England for his funeral, she couldn't remember from one day to the next what was happening. He lay in state in St George's Chapel, Windsor, and though she attended the ceremony on the first day, each succeeding day would say, vaguely, 'I really must go and see David lying in state. . . .' Unkind people attribute her loss of memory to the fact that her face was lifted once too often. It is apparently true that her permanent plastic surgeon refused to perform surgery again, saying it would be too dangerous. She then went to an unscrupulous doctor, who operated, causing pressure on the brain, it is said. I don't believe this story, but it is typical of the vitriolic gossip rife in café society. I hope she was not surrounded by vultures, waiting for the kill, like Barbara.

Aunt Bridget worked for years with Edward Molyneux in his dress shop. He was renowned for his meanness, but for advertising's sake he would lend dresses and fur coats to Bridget because she moved in all the best circles. One winter he let her wear a very beautiful leopard-skin coat. She knew it would be taken back at any moment, so took no care of it, flung it on the floor, never bothered to brush it and never hung it up.

One morning, arriving at the shop, Edward said, 'Bridget darling, I'd like to make you a present of that leopard coat.' She was staggered, and when the lunch-hour came, she raced back to her flat, and, as she said, 'I picked it up, stroked it, brushed it, fed it and hung it up in the cupboard, but it was too late, darling, I'd mistreated it once too often.'

She lived to be an old lady and came here to the Minzah Hotel with her son and his mistress and a grandson. She had had her face lifted so many times that it was like a mask; she couldn't close her eyes when she slept. 'I went again the other day, darling, to have it done once more, but my little woman around the corner said, "I'm sorry, Lady Victor, but there's nothing left to lift."'

She had been left a very valuable diamond necklace by her two maiden aunts. When she wasn't wearing it, it was in her handbag. She wouldn't move without it. 'My insurance, darling,' she said.

I once gave a dinner party for her. She arrived in a flowing green chiffon dress – lovely, but too *décolletée* and far too young for a woman in her eighties. The painted face was stretched to bursting-point; the hair dyed deep raspberry was sadly thin and done in the style of the twenties. Her appearance was really terrifying, and my Tangier friends were amazed and frightened by this inhuman apparition. Her opening lines on arrival were, 'My little grandson fell into the Minzah swimming-pool this morning. I was too blind to see it, and my son was too busy with his mistress to notice. Fortunately a kind American gentleman fished him out and brought him to me – alive, but much the worse for wear.'

Michael Duff came regularly to stay with me. One summer recently friends gave a fancy-dress ball. Michael wore a caftan that was far too short for his immense height, and a turban with a three-foot-long peacock's feather soaring upwards from it. He looked a joke; but notwithstanding, he was so handsome that a young Peruvian fell in love with him and followed in his wake wherever he went. Michael spent most of the evening running away from him, and in his execrable French saying, 'Pas ce soir, peut-être demain.' This had no effect, as the young man did not speak French. The next morning, when Michael came down to breakfast, Ira Belline, Boul de Breteuil and I were already at the table. He entered the dining-room singing, 'J'ai deux amours – mon pays et Perou!'

Each morning Michael went to the town beach, which is always crowded. He disliked empty beaches. He would paddle rather than swim, then go for a walk dressed in very abbreviated shorts, a towel wrapped round his shoulders, and a peaked linen cap worn very much on one side. He said that all the 'mauvais garçons' laughed at him, but he didn't mind. In reply to their laughter he would say, 'Bonjour monsieur'.

One evening Michael was sitting next to a drunk man at the Parade Bar. He was nervous, as the man appeared very aggressive. He surreptitiously edged his bar-stool further away. The man said, 'What the hell is the matter with you? I won't bite.' Michael replied, 'You might.'

Michael was unable to reverse a car, for he could not turn his head as he always had a stiff neck. This made parking doubly difficult, and either the front or the back of the car would stick well out in the middle of the road. Once when the police remonstrated with him, he gave his charming smile and said, 'Pardon, monsieur, je suis un fou anglais – parquez la voiture pour moi et je serai très content.'

When I have written about my cousin Michael, I have seldom mentioned the serious side of his life. For years he lived at the foot of the Welsh mountains, where he bore the responsibility of being a large landowner. He was Lord Lieutenant of Carnarvon and head of the St John of Jerusalem organization, and he served as Mayor of Carnarvon. He worked tirelessly for better conditions, for the welfare of the men and their families who had laboured for generations, father to son, in his slate quarries at Llanberis. It was a sad moment when they closed down (there was little demand for slate, and the quarry was losing money each year). The reception Michael got when he visited the quarries, which he often did, was touching. He would spend hours listening and talking to the quarrymen, trying to organize outings and means to alleviate their hard jobs. Tuberculosis was rampant in the old days, owing to the slate dust that got into the lungs. Michael would arrange for the bad cases to be sent where the air was cleaner and purer.

It seems strange to me that Michael – who devoted himself to public life in Wales, and, incidentally, received the Queen and the entire royal family at Vaynol during the investiture of the Prince of Wales, as well as having his Park cluttered up with the royal horses and carriages and tents for the soldiers – never received any sort of decoration. So many people are decorated for so much less than

Michael's efforts for his country over a period of some forty-five years.

On one of his annual visits to Morocco, Michael Duff brought with him his faithful valet Edward, who had been ill. Michael thought that a change would do him good. I joined them in Marrakesh to find Edward miserable, for he had taken an instant dislike to it. After Edward had suffered three days of acute depression, Michael sent him back to England. Edward could not adapt himself to the East and was too nervous to walk through the souks, even with a guide. Another complaint was that there were no other visiting valets or ladies' maids for him to talk to. 'Now, if only Miss Suckling were here, Sir Michael, I would be all right.'

Miss Suckling had been Beatrice Guinness's maid. Beatrice was a great friend of ours and a frequent visitor to Vaynol, Michael's home in Wales. On her death, Suckling went to Queen Elizabeth, the Queen Mother, with whom she remained until she retired a few years ago. I once asked her if she enjoyed working at Clarence House. 'Oh yes, sir, Her Majesty is wonderful, but there was no one like Mrs Guinness' was her reply.

Suckling was right. Beatrice was one of the most entertaining people I have ever met. Her remarks were original and unexpected, as when Osbert Sitwell went up to her in the foyer of the Ritz and said, 'Good morning, Beatrice, I met a friend of yours yesterday. . . .' Before he could finish the sentence, Beatrice retorted, 'Impossible, I have no friends.'

One day she asked me to go with her to buy a new hat. As she entered the shop the owner came forward and said, 'What can I do for you, Mrs Guinness?'

'I want a hat for a middle-aged woman whose husband simply loathes her.'

Her husband had a mistress whom, naturally, Beatrice resented. That same day after lunch, she said, 'I must talk to Dick', picked up the telephone, dialled a number and said, 'This is Mrs Guinness speaking. Will you tell your mistress, who is my husband's mistress, that his wife would like to speak to him.'

I remember Michael and I sitting on each side of Beatrice at her dressing-table whilst she was doing her hair and making up her face. This finished, she put on her wonderful emerald and diamond drop earrings. Michael said, 'How extraordinary, Beatrice. I never noticed before that one earring is longer than the other.'

'Nor had I,' she replied. 'Which one do you prefer?'

'Oh, the longer one,' said Michael. With that she threw the short one out of the window.

Her house in Great Cumberland Place was bombed during the war and Beatrice was buried under the rubble. As her daughter Zita was frantically trying to get to her, removing all the debris she could, a voice from under commanded, 'Zita, don't blow on your mother. Anyway, this is not your job. Get the air-raid warden.'

When the Queen Mother paid a visit the next day, Beatrice was sitting on the front doorstep in her mink coat and with the inevitable rope of pearls. She said, 'Don't bother about me, Your Majesty. Go to what is left of the back door, for my cook used to be kitchenmaid at Glamis.'

For Christmas 1979 I stayed in England with my niece and nephew, Maria Carmella and Harry, at Hambleden. Michael was there. The dreaded cancer had returned and we knew that he had a very short time left. It was not the gayest of reunions. My sister and I then took him to stay with my sister-in-law Mary Pembroke at Wilton for the New Year.

New Year's Eve was spent with Cecil Beaton, who in spite of the stroke he had suffered three years before, was in high spirits. During the evening he said to me, 'Poor Michael, I'd much rather be half paralysed like I am than have what he has. I can still enjoy my food, my drink, and laugh as much as I ever did, whereas Michael seems unable to enjoy anything.' But within three weeks Cecil was dead.

I was the first person Cecil had visited abroad after his stroke. He arrived in Tangier with his faithful friend and secretary Eileen Hose, in a wheelchair. On seeing me he burst into tears and did so off and on for the first week. I decided that too many people in England had said 'Poor Cecil' and treated him as a hopeless invalid, so one morning I told him, 'For God's sake, Kek, stop blubbing. You could be blind or deaf or gaga or unable to speak. You're none of those things, so get out into the garden and try to draw with your left hand.'

He was astounded. Eileen was sent into town to buy the necessary equipment, and Cecil set to work. By the end of the visit he had done some charming sketches which were later published in *Vogue*. The blubbing ceased and his morale grew steadily better. When he left, he was attempting photography again. One day he was photographing Marjorie Tweeddale, and Eileen was holding the camera for him. I knew he was on the mend when he shouted, 'Eileen, get your great fat fist out of the lens!' This marked the start of his recovery, and he went from strength to strength till the day he died.

Cecil was not a happy man; very few ambitious men are. From an early age he was determined to become famous, but how to achieve this ambition he was not sure. Photography started him on his climb to fame and in a short time he was considered the best photographer in England, subsequently in America and eventually world wide. Cecil was not satisfied with what he considered a minor art. He wanted to go much further. This he achieved by sheer hard work and driving ambition.

His flamboyant appearance and special way of talking were more a publicity act than the real Cecil. To be noticed and talked about was part of his plan and all-important to his future; in fact to be in the public eye. I remember driving him in my car from Salzburg to Budapest. He was dressed like the Emperor Franz Josef. On arrival at the Dina Palova Hotel, I am ashamed to say that I was so embarrassed by his appearance that I said, 'You go on in and see about the rooms, as I think I've got some engine trouble and had better take the car straight to the garage.'

This flamboyance showed also in the decoration of his houses in the early days. At that time he was not rich, but he had a remarkable flair for picking up rubbish and making it look like something special. For instance, at Ashcombe, his first country house, the curtains were made of brown hessian, on to which he had sewn thousands of mother-of-pearl buttons, the effect of which was fascinating and original. He acquired nondescript tables and chairs, which he painted white with dozens of different coloured cushions, there were a few plaster statuettes scattered about, jardinières filled with pot plants, a birdcage acting as a chandelier, huge sofas, white sheepskin rugs and great vases of flowers cunningly lit from behind. The effect was theatrical, perhaps a little tawdry, but extremely eye-catching.

None of this flamboyance came from lack of taste, for later Cecil bought beautiful things from all over the world, things of real value such as two lovely sphinxes on marble bases which he bequeathed to me in his will. He preferred French furniture and *objets d'art* to anything else. Paris was where he collected most of his precious possessions.

Cecil was a brilliant conversationalist, and whether you were alone with him or with a group, you knew an evening spent in his company would be stimulating and amusing. I don't think many people really knew him. He showed the world the side he wanted them to see, the rather brittle, sophisticated and hard side. Underneath this façade, he was kind, generous and deeply sensitive, easily hurt and quite often in floods of tears. Devoted to his mother, his aunts and his sisters, he helped them in every way possible, his mother and aunts to move in higher circles, his sisters to make good marriages. I think that, of all his family, his Aunt Jessie, of whom he wrote a biography called *My Bolivian Aunt*, was the only one who understood him. She had travelled the world, married an ambassador, and as she once said to me, after Mrs Beaton had been very rude to her in my presence, and I said, 'How dare she talk to you like that!': 'You must pity poor Ettie. I have danced with all the crowned and monarchical heads of Europe, and Ettie gets a tremendous kick if the Duchess of Kent comes to tea.' When Cecil was a schoolboy she took him to the theatre and showered him with programmes and play pictorials. It was through her encouragement that Cecil started his artistic career.

Cecil's drawings may not be the work of a great artist, but they have an individuality and a lightness of touch which makes them very attractive and decorative. The likenesses he achieved were remarkable, and many a not so beautiful woman became a beauty without the drawing losing its fundamental likeness.

Cecil had immense courage and great energy. The first thirty years of his life were a real struggle. It was his brilliance in designing clothes and scenery for the theatre that was his greatest achievement, and even then he was not satisfied. He longed to be a great painter and a great playwright. His fame has doubled since his death. As Oscar Wilde said, 'No one is really famous till after they are dead.' He fell in love like everyone else, but never quite enough to curb his ambition. For example, if he was having an affair with someone in London and he was offered a job in America, he would up stakes and be off without a moment's hesitation. This sounds callous, but to be a success was just that much more important to Cecil than being in love. A character like Cecil's does not make for happiness.

The recent biography by Hugo Vickers is a disappointment to me. He depicts Cecil almost entirely as a social-climbing snob. This is unfair, but then Vickers met him only once, and some of Cecil's so-called friends whom he interviewed were not really fond of him. So many of his real friends are dead. Clarissa Avon and my sister-in-law, Mary Pembroke, are still with us, but the list of those who are not is too long to quote. Those not really fond of him were amused by him, fascinated by him, and perhaps some were jealous of him. Others laughed at him behind his back, but nevertheless they all wanted to be in his orbit. Most of his real friends were intellectuals. Not that I count myself as one, being an ordinary friend of his when we were both in our twenties, but surely he must have been thought worthwhile to be close to people like Tchelitchew, Bebi Gerard, Cocteau, the Sitwells, among many other brilliant people. Naturally, as his bread and butter came from his photographs, he sought out the most sought-after subjects: the royal family, leading society hostesses, famous film stars, great actors and actresses of the theatre, diplomats, ambassadors and their wives and children. This was not snobbery but the means to an end. I must add here that the latter part of the biography is kinder and more tolerant.

Perhaps the side of his character that people found most disturbing was his taking violent dislikes to people, sometimes for no apparent reason, and with acid wit and often venomous tongue he could destroy them. I think this often came from his being over-tired. He worked himself literally to death, and I suspect his stroke came about because he never let up and drove himself harder and harder, which is all very well when you are young but disastrous when you reach Cecil's age.

I am sure that his loyal, loving secretary Eileen, whose selfless devotion and affection helped him through so many years, would have agreed with what I have written if she were still alive. Cecil was one of my dearest friends, and I miss him continually. Often when something funny, strange or extraordinary happens, I think, 'Oh I do wish Cecil was here to share it with me. It will certainly be a long time, if ever, before Cecil is forgotten – his diaries alone will ensure that.

My beloved cousin, Caroline Duff, was a frequent visitor to Tangier. Caroline was made for love, and she suffered more than most people in life because of the deaths of those she loved. As a girl she was sheer enchantment. Everyone was in love with Caroline. She possessed a rare quality of warmth, physical attraction and deep understanding. Men and women alike were bowled over by her unique qualities.

Her first love was Antony Knebworth, son of Lord Lytton, who had worshipped Caroline since she was twelve years old. When she was eighteen, he asked her to marry him. She had seen nothing of the world and refused, saying, 'I must be given time to meet people and see what life is like away from the schoolroom.'

Antony was killed in May 1933 while practising formation flying at Hendon with his squadron of the RAF, for a display to be given before the Prince of Wales. Caroline was stunned and miserable. This feeling was aggravated by Antony's mother, Lady Lytton, who never ceased telling Caroline that if she had married Antony, at least he would have had a few happy moments with her. This was a thoughtless thing to say. At each anniversary of his death, Lady Lytton would insist on taking Caroline to visit his grave.

Caroline then studied for the stage and worked in repertory companies all over the country. She made a name for herself and appeared with Fay Compton in a successful London production. During this time she was in love with Rex Whistler, the painter. The war broke out, Rex joined the Welsh Guards and Caroline the Mobile Canteens Service. Rex was killed at Demouville, near Caen, in July 1944.

Caroline had made many new friends during her days in the theatre, the most important being Audrey Carton, who many years before had written a play with Sir Gerald du Maurier called *The Dancers*. It was in this play that Tallulah Bankhead made her first London appearance. As we all know, Tallulah went from strength to strength and became one of the most famous actresses of that period. Audrey faded into the background as a figure in the theatre, but owing to her beauty, intelligence and caustic wit remained a great personality in that particular world.

She was a bad influence on Caroline: they set up house together in Panelton Square. Caroline drifted away from her own world and, apart from the family, saw only a small group of friends, chiefly women. I suspect that Audrey was the real love of her life, though she had many affairs with men. Eventually she married my cousin, Michael Duff. This was an arrangement beneficial to both.

The last ten years of her life were probably the happiest, owing to her friendship with Marguerite McBey. It was a genuine *amitié amoureuse* – two ladies of a certain age finding a haven in friendship. Caroline, who practically never left England, started travelling. Marguerite is an inveterate traveller, and together they covered a large part of the globe, Marguerite painting exquisite water-colours, and she and Caroline poring over the diaries of Marguerite's husband, James McBey, whose autobiography they edited.

When Caroline was desperately ill, and there was no hope of recovery, Marguerite went to London to see her in hospital. She returned sad and shaken; she told me that Caroline was peaceful and calm and talked bluntly about death, saying she was quite prepared for it. She looked beautiful and serene. When Marguerite left her, she said 'Au revoir', and Caroline nodded, meaning, 'I'm sure, but in the next world.'

My cousin Elizabeth von Hofmannsthal was the younger sister of Caroline Duff. She had a heart-breaking time for two years, nursing first her husband Raimund and then her sister Caroline through the same hideous illness until they both died. In spite of this she remained beautiful as ever, though there was now a wounded look in her eyes which had not been there before. She was as courageous as she was lovely, and to an outsider never changed. Liz was deeply emotional inside, but had the restraint which flows in the Paget blood – not showing feelings to the general public. We were very close to each other; she once told me that she had spent half her life in tears.

Raimund was Austrian, son of the great Hugo von Hofmann-sthal, and a man of great charm and intelligence. His gaiety was infectious. If Raimund was staying for a weekend or was a guest at dinner, both functions were sure to be an unqualified success. His appreciation and enthusiasm for beautiful objects, building, music, theatre and ballet was immense. He had the same appreciation for beautiful women, good food and first-class wine. Once at the Savoy Grill we were ordering supper. Raimund looked at the menu and said, 'Ve vill have a glass of vodka, zen voodcock and ze vite vine zat ze vife likes.' Liz exclaimed, 'There goes the housekeeping money for this week.' With Liz's beauty and bubbling humour and Raimund's extrovert qualities, it is no wonder that they once were the most sought-after couple in England.

Liz visited Morocco twice. The first time was some eighteen years ago. She had been here only for a short time and had seen nothing of the country, so we decided to drive into the interior. Our first stop was Meknes. There we stayed two nights, the second being the most important night during Ramadan. Hamid Nuamani, a Moroccan friend, took us out after dinner. The town was packed. The woman were dressed in their party clothes, with wonderful coloured caftans, the Berber women from the hills wearing their splendid mountain finery. The streets were decorated and lit with hundreds of twinkling lights. Hamid took us to the tomb of Moulay Ismael, constructed in the middle of a huge mosque and now open to everyone. The crowd was so enormous that we only got half-way to the tomb. We decided to give up, as we were packed like sardines – for several moments the crush was truly frightening. Having eventually reached the car, I realized that my driving spectacles, cigarette-lighter and -holder had gone. They had not been stolen, but as I was wearing a sweater with shallow pockets, they must have fallen out among the jostling crowd. I was in despair, as we had many miles to drive before getting back to Tangier. As it turned out, it was a blessing in disguise, as I found out that I could see perfectly well without my spectacles. It was only laziness that had made me wear them.

The next day we went to Marrakesh, passing through a lovely bit of country where the King Ranch is situated. It is not King Hassan's ranch, as is so often supposed; rather, the bulls and cows have been imported from the King Ranch in America in order to renew and improve the existing breed of cattle in Morocco. The project has been so successful in the last ten years that there are now thousands of cattle. It is a remarkable sight, driving for thirty or forty miles on a new macadam road through unspoilt countryside with not even a telegraph or an electric-light pole to be seen, whilst on each side of the road these healthy, splendid beasts are grazing contentedly on rich pasture.

Marrakesh was a disappointment. The Hotel Mamounia had only a skeleton staff because of Ramadan. There were a great many more tourists than they had expected. It took an hour to get breakfast, the air-conditioning did not work, nor did half the lights in the bedrooms. The heat, although it was the end of September, was as midsummer, so we left after two nights.

We went on to Essaouira, a lovely eighteenth-century town built on a rocky promontory that juts into the sea. As well as an excellent fish restaurant on the beach, and bracing Atlantic air, there is a submerged city a few hundred yards out. Essaouira is different from other Moroccan cities in that the architect was a Frenchman taken prisoner by the sultan of the time, who, with great intelligence, instead of keeping him in gaol, put him to work designing a new town. The result is enchanting: the harbour is grand with crenellated octagonal towers, and there is a beautiful arch through which fishing-boats can pass. The town on the sea side is protected by broad ramparts with circular look-out towers at various points. These ramparts are as broad as the average street; thirty people abreast could pass along them. The Hotel des Îles is comfortable and built in the same style and colour as the town, so that it blends perfectly. We stayed three nights, walking along the ramparts, swimming and picnicking. A few years later Liz died, also of cancer like her husband and sister.

Annie Nutting, well known as the best and most beautiful of the English models in the late fifties and sixties, retired to marry Sir Anthony Nutting who, as Under-Secretary for Foreign Affairs, had resigned over Suez. He refused to re-enter politics, and has since written several books: *The Arabs*, *Lawrence of Arabia* and lives of General Gordon of Khartoum and President Nasser of Egypt. The Nuttings built a house here on a lovely piece of land at Cap Spartel. As the house had no light or telephone, Anthony would not allow Annie to stay there without him, so she often stayed with me when he was unable to come out to Tangier with her. They have since sold the house.

We have made many trips to the south together. During one particular journey we were accompanied by Annie and Tony Pawson. One day we had driven a great many miles and finally arrived in Tinerhir. There the hotel manager said that there had been a telephone message to say that my brother Sidney had died. The manager gave the message to Tony instead of me. Annie wisely decided not to say anything that evening, as there was nothing that we could do – no post office and no way of getting back to civilization to catch a plane. The next morning they told me. We motored on until we came to Ouarzazate, where I sent telegrams to the family, but it was not until we reached Marrakesh that I could telephone my sister-in-law. By this time Sidney had already been buried, so we continued the trip. Tony and Annie wanted to see Tiznit and Goulimine.

I am reminded of a story. Tony, Annie and I were staying in Taroudant a few years ago. Annie was beautiful, Tony very good-looking, and I was not too bad for my age. Also staying in the hotel was a handsome, distinguished-looking Moroccan. He could not take his eyes off Annie. He made polite passes at her; Annie equally politely brushed them aside. The gentleman must have thought, I expect that one of these gentlemen is her husband. He then found we had three separate bedrooms and was so intrigued by this that he asked about the set-up.

'We are just old friends,' I replied.

'But who is sleeping with whom?' he wanted to know.

'No one is sleeping with anyone. As I said, we are just old friends.'

'Ah, I see – you are all three sleeping together. May I join you?'

It was impossible for him to realize that there could be friendship between a man and a woman without sex, unless it was a very close relationship. However, in spite of his not understanding the situation, we became friends and had drinks together. No one slept with anyone, but it was not for want of trying on his side. Annie firmly locked her door; Tony and I had no need to, as without her we were not much fun.

Annie and Tony had been gossiping away in the back of the car for hours. It is a long drive almost to the edge of the desert and I was tired. The great walls of Tiznit appeared. My companions were still talking, so I stopped the car and said, 'I've brought you

71

two thousand miles to see Tiznit. Will you kindly stop chattering about the Duchess of Windsor's latest hair-style and *look*.'

We then picnicked in a fig grove, drank a lot of red wine and fell asleep. After leaving Tiznit we drove on to Goulimine, where there is the great camel market every Sunday. Thousands of camels come in from the desert with their masters, who are called the 'blue men' because they are veiled with blue material like the women, to keep the sand from entering their mouths and noses. It is a magical sight, for the light is extraordinary in that part of the world; and all the different shades of blues that the women and men wear – some bright, some pale, some faded, some mottled, moving against the multitude of camels – are unforgettable.

The hotel was primitive; the hot water was seldom hot; and the lights went out at ten o'clock; the loos never flushed. But for one night, none of this mattered. I am told that now the hotel is much improved and am looking forward to my next visit.

Alice Delysia, the French actress and singer who was at the height of her fame in the late twenties and early thirties, was a friend of Charles B. Cochran, the great impresario, and appeared in many of his revues and musical comedies. Her most famous and, I think, the show that had the longest run, was *Mother of Pearl*. Alice retired from the stage when she married Admiral Colne Bernard of the French Navy. He, on his own retirement, joined the Foreign Service, and Alice became the hostess of the French Consul-General in Valencia. She and her husband came frequently to Tangier for their holidays and Alice had hardly changed – the same gay, vital woman she was in the twenties.

One evening at the Hermitage Restaurant in Tangier she stood up after dinner and with no accompaniment sang the score of *Mother of Pearl* in the clear, pure voice of a twenty-year-old girl. It was miraculous and the other diners cheered her (with the refrain?).

Alice was always full of fun. I remember at a theatrical supper party we played the kissing game, in which one person is blindfolded and sits on a chair whilst all the others in the room come up and give him or her a really juicy kiss on the mouth. Alice was blindfolded and my turn came to kiss her. After the kiss was over, she gasped and exclaimed, 'It is David, it is David. His mouth is just like his father's.'

Long afterwards I asked my father, 'Daddy, did you ever have an affair with Delysia?'

'Good God, old boy, how on earth did you know that? Yes I did, and I've never forgotten it.'

On one occasion Moira Fraser, the actress, and her husband Roger Lubbock were staying with me. At the same time, my cousin Veronica Tennant had staying with her Laura and John Arundel, her daughter and son-in-law. John is an ardent Catholic, and one evening was holding forth on the subject, about what a wonderful religion it is. He was young and in a mild way trying to convert us.

The following day, we all went to bathe at Robinson Plage, a lonely, isolated restaurant-bar on the Atlantic coast. On arriving Roger said, 'Damn, I've left my bathing trunks behind.'

I said, 'I'm not going to drive all the way home to fetch them. Try and borrow a pair from the management.'

Moira and I plunged into the sea. As we emerged, Roger came down the beach to meet us attired for swimming. 'Isn't it lucky?' he cried. 'John Arundel had a second pair.'

'Yes,' retorted Moira. 'But I do hope you don't catch Catholicism.'

In the 1950s Bryce Nairn was Minister at our Legation. He and his wife Margaret were much loved, and they remained here seven years, owing to the influence of Winston Churchill, a great friend. Margaret was a first-rate painter in water-colours. During the winter Winston spent several weeks each year in Marrakesh, and he and Margaret would take a picnic out into the surrounding country and paint all day.

Bryce was born in Marrakesh. They owned a charming house in the Palmerie, four and a half miles outside the town, so it was eminently suitable that they should retire from Tangier without being posted elsewhere. During Bryce's residency here, Winston and his wife would sometimes come and stay, she at the Legation and he at an hotel, as by that time he could not manage the Legation's stairs, and there was no lift.

One evening I was dining with the Nairns when the telephone

rang to say that Winston, Clemmie and their party were landing at Tangier airport any minute. Owing to an electric storm, it was impossible to land in Gibraltar, where they were joining the Onassis yacht. Bryce rushed to the airport, officials were alerted and accommodation in an hotel arranged for the party, which consisted of not fewer than eight people. The aircraft had been circling round for a long time trying to land at Gibraltar, and eventually had been rerouted to Tangier.

When they arrived at the Legation, we were in the drawing-room and Clemmie, beautiful and immaculate, sailed into the room saying, 'Oh dear, oh dear, the poor darling Nairns – here we are descending on them like a lot of wounded ducks.'

The following day the Onassis yacht arrived from Gibraltar to pick them up. We lunched on board. I had known Tina Onassis for some time. The party was gay and the luxury of the yacht extraordinary – hardly one's idea of a boat, but very much one's idea of what the very rich would want. We left at four o'clock and went back to the roof of the Legation to watch the yacht sail through the Strait of Gibraltar into the Mediterranean.

I had known the Churchills all my life, as they were regular guests at Wilton, being friends of my mother and father. They spent time each Whitsuntide with us, and my mother rechristened it 'Winstontide'. There was, however, a slight falling-off as Winston switched from one political party to another, and my father, president of the Primrose League organization of young Tories, was too often heckled at meetings about Churchill's change of heart. When my mother attacked Winston on this subject, he replied, 'My dear Bee, you must remember that a politician's personal ambition almost always outweighs his political judge-ment.' It is remarkable that his loyal, beautiful, splendid wife was a Liberal all her life and remained one to the end of her days.

Another Greek millionaire, Niarchos, would also spend a few days here in his yacht from time to time. I infinitely preferred his boat; it was less spectacular, less garish, and done up with good taste. The wives of these two giant shipping magnates, Tina and Eugenia, were sisters. Tina married and divorced the Marquess of Blandford. She was an ambitious girl, left him and married her by then dead sister's husband, Niarchos. I loved Eugenia – she was simple, beautiful and really only liked life in the country with her children. This she seldom got, for her husband was a social man.

In those days many yachts called at Tangier, but now only a few do. Seymour Camrose is a regular visitor. He comes with a party of friends, all of whom are friends of mine, including Joan, Princess Ali Khan, who acts as his hostess. Two years ago Joan and Seymour got married and spent their honeymoon here in Tangier.

Joan is English, the daughter of Lord Churston, a childhood friend of mine. She has had an interesting life being the mother of the present Aga Khan. When her husband, Prince Ali Khan died, Joan was left to bring up this boy and his younger brother according to their faith. She has travelled extensively with them wherever the Aga has his followers – Pakistan, India, Afghanistan. He is now married to a beautiful English wife who works as hard as Joan did to help her husband in his religious life.

The Droghedas, Joan and Garrett, were regulars on Seymour's yacht. Garrett and I were at Eton together and kept up our friendship through the years. (So often school friends disappear completely.) Garrett's father was a friend of my family; in fact, as mentioned earlier, he married as his second wife my aunt Olive (Lady Victor Paget), well known on the stage as Olive May. She had married my uncle Victor when very young. He was a charming rogue, as she soon found out. When she divorced him and married Lord Drogheda, not only did Garrett and I spend our schooldays together, but most of the summer holidays. Little did I think that my old school chum would become so prominent, Managing Director of *The Financial Times* and Chairman of the Board of Covent Garden. The climax came when he received the Garter from the Queen, the highest decoration you can acquire. Joan was a considerable pianist, beautiful, intelligent, bubbling with humour. Until her debilitating illness overtook her she gave concerts twice a year with great success. They lived in a delightful house off the gardens on the edge of Windsor Great Park. Garrett was an expert gardener and made a romantic and lovely setting for them both. He came here to stay with me one summer without Joan, who was practising for a recital. He was overworked, tired and nervous, so she had written me suggesting he visit on his own. Tangier is a relaxing place, and he enjoyed two weeks of swimming and lying in the sun.

Joan Drogheda died on 16 December 1989, and Garrett died eight days later.

When Princess Alexandra and Angus Ogilvy came over from Spain, I gave a lunch for them. They were on their honeymoon and had been stared at so much by the Spaniards that they decided to come incognito as 'Mr and Mrs Twitt'. I told my luncheon guests that they were coming, but they didn't believe me, so no one dressed up. Not that the Ogilvys would have wanted them to, but the guests were mortified not to be wearing their Sunday best.

After lunch I took them around the Casbah. Unfortunately, in the harbour of Tangier was an English ship carrying British tourists who were on shore for the day. We met a group of them in the Place de la Casbah. Of course they recognized Princess Alexandra – and she was wonderful. The tourists wanted so much to take a photograph of the happy couple and asked if they could. Princess Alexandra said, smiling, 'Of course you can, but on one condition – that you promise not to recognize us again and don't tell any of the rest of your ship's passengers that we are here.'

She and Angus then posed for the tourists, who were in raptures. They kept their word, however, for wherever we met them during the rest of the day, they tactfully turned their heads the other way.

Noël Coward came here for a few days, but it was not warm enough for him so he moved south. This was a disappointment, as I had seen very little of him in recent years; in fact, not since we had both become expatriates. In the old days my life was involved with his through my friendship with Jack Wilson. I stayed many weekends at Goldenhurst, the farm Noël had bought on the Romney Marsh in Kent. When the barn was converted into what was called 'the big room', Jack and I decorated it; and we travelled many hundreds of miles scouring the countryside for suitable antique furniture. Noël was always charming to me, though I was an interloper in the magic circle that surrounded him. His mother and father and his unmarried aunt Vida lived in the old part of the house, but we all had meals together. Mr Coward was a tiresome man; Mrs

Coward a courageous battle axe; Aunt Vida resembled a little field mouse.

I remember one night Noël asked me what I thought of a new white wine which, unknown to him, his father had bought. I said that I preferred the wine we had drunk the previous weekend. Mr Coward banged his hand on the table, rose to his feet and stamped out of the room saying, 'This wine is streets ahead of Graves!'

Another incident which remains engraved on my memory concern Adrienne Allen, a constant visitor to Goldenhurst and loved by everyone. One weekend Aunt Vida was absent (she was staying with her sister-in-law) and we missed her. The following weekend Adrienne said to Vida, 'How we missed you last weekend!'

'I'm glad to hear it,' said Aunt Vida.

'Yes,' continued Adrienne. 'You are like a dear little brown leaf rustling around the house.'

'Little brown leaf, indeed,' replied Aunt Vida. 'Thank you for nothing, Miss Allen!'

Noël was the kindest of men beneath the brittle exterior. His patience and thoughtfulness with his family was touching. He admired and loved his mother, and tolerated his father. Aunt Vida was his favourite aunt, although she kept herself very much in the background. Mr Coward's sister, Aunt Ida, lived nearby in Folkestone. I didn't like her much and she certainly didn't like me. The first time we met, I had no idea where she lived. During polite conversation she asked me which town I preferred – Folkestone or Littlestone, the town nearest to Goldenhurst. I replied, thinking that I was being tactful, 'Oh, Littlestone, of course.'

'Do you really, Mr Herbert? I happen to live in Folkestone, and it has a far superior front.'

Some years ago an elderly English beauty known as the 'Iced Orchid' came to Tangier with a woman friend who was as unexotic as the former was exotic. It was August and very hot. One day we were sitting in deck-chairs after lunching at a restaurant by the sea. The 'Iced Orchid' dozed off, and I happened to look in her direction. To my amazement I saw rivulets of liquid make-up running down her face, revealing squares of transparent sticking-plaster holding up the sagging skin. I nudged her friend who, horrified, woke up the beauty and hurried her away to the bathing cabin. Half an hour later she reappeared, exquisitely made up, wearing a pink chiffon handkerchief tied around her chin with a huge black picture hat perched on top.

A certain English peer, whose mother was a friend of mine, disliked me. The feeling was mutual. He drank a lot and was a barfly, staying up all night in the various bars around town. One evening he went too far. He loosed off several rounds of ammunition from his revolver in a respectable club where people were dancing. The police were called and he was taken to prison, where he spent several nights. On one of those nights he was supposed to dine at our Consulate, so his brother sent a message saying that he was indisposed. When he came out of prison, a friend asked him what it had been like. He replied, 'Oh fine, just like any other, but the time always passes in a flash, because in every gaol I have visited, I have kept busy carving deep into the walls the words, *David Herbert slept here*.'

Count Charles de Breteuil, owner of the French newspapers during the Protectorate, invited most of the British colony to a cocktail party given at the offices of his newspaper here in Tangier. The invitation read: 'To have the honour to meet a member of the Royal Family.' This caused a great deal of excitement. Who could it be? It was summer and the guests came dressed in their best party clothes, wearing flowered or feathered hats. One woman got very drunk and was carried out early in the proceedings. The guests waited: no sign of the mysterious royal person. It was getting late, and eventually someone asked Charles if the guest of honour was not coming. Charles replied, 'But she's been and gone.' It was a hoax. The drunk lady was the sister of the wife of one of the Queen Mother's nephews. He had married his nurse.

Ed, Lord Stanley of Alderley, liked Tangier and would visit us from time to time on his small yacht. His first wife was my cousin,

Audrey Talbot, but since then he has had several other wives. His last was a rich lady of a different world. Ed brought her to Tangier and said, 'David, she is awfully nice but awfully common. I know you will like her.'

Ed was his usual tough, outspoken self, so when he introduced me to her, he said, 'Here she is. I warned you she was common, but don't let that bother you. She's a jolly good sort.' I was embarrassed, but the wife took it well. I imagine she was accustomed to this form of introduction.

We lunched together with several other friends, and Lady Stanley at one moment said 'Pardon'. Ed shouted across the table. 'You promised me you'd stop saying "Pardon" if I stopped saying "Fuck"!'

Several years running after the last war Sir Claude Russell, ex-British Ambassador and member of the Bedford family, visited Gibraltar with Lady Russell during the winter months for health reasons. His wife, Athenais, was tall, handsome and Greek. She was a well-known botanist, erudite and intelligent, though she drove one mad with her high, affected, complaining voice. She was amusing if you laughed at her; this she didn't mind, which was endearing.

'Oh, Claud, Claud,' she would cry, clambering up a muddy bank. 'I've found a little blue squill – come quickly.'

'I can't and won't come quickly. What's the hurry? It can't run away,' he would reply.

Diana Cooper had a golden spaniel puppy, as yet unnamed; he had very long, floppy ears. Every name we thought of was rejected. It was spring and we were walking in the garden. As we passed beneath a golden weeping willow, its trailing branches just bursting into bud, Athenais cried, 'Diana, I've got it. Willow, willow, willow.' The dog was named Willow!

Gibraltar bored them, as did Spain, so they would frequently come over to Tangier. They stayed at the best hotel and entertained us all in princely fashion. At that time money restrictions were tight. It was virtually impossible to get money out of Gibraltar.

One day I said, 'Sir Claud, how do you manage for money?'

'Ah, David,' he said. 'Look at me – tall, sad-looking and old – an ex-ambassador without a stain on his character, wearing a black Homburg hat, carrying a beautifully rolled umbrella, and accompanied by a charming wife – a picture of respectability. When we arrive at the hotel and go to our room, Athenais unpacks. But I unroll my umbrella.'

Alvilde Lees-Milne, wife of Jim Lees-Milne, a shining light of the National Trust for many years and an historian and writer, came to visit. My nephew Henry Pembroke and his wife Claire, who had motored from Marrakesh, joined us at Erfoud.

The next morning we drove to Merzuga. I had been there many times before, but it was their first visit. It was a glorious morning, still, without a cloud in the sky. No proper road exists to Merzuga; there is only a piste and it is easy to get lost if there is a wind, as the sand quickly covers the stones marking the way. It is for this reason that I always take a guide.

One the way there, we left the piste and went across open desert to where they were quarrying slabs of marble in which are embedded fossilized shells and fish. They polish the slabs and make coffee-tables with them, all beautiful and each unique. As we watched this fascinating operation a slight breeze arose. The guide looked at the sky and said that we had better move on in case it developed into a sandstorm.

We drove off. Barely three minutes had passed before we were blinded by sand. The wind got stronger and stronger; we could not see more than a few feet ahead. I slowed down.

The guide said, 'What are you slowing down for? There is nothing here to run into. Drive as fast as you can till we reach the piste – before the sand obliterates the stones.'

I obeyed; we were in his hands. I said, 'How do you know where the piste is?'

He replied, 'We who are born here have a nose for the desert. Just follow my directions – now a little more to the left, straight on, now to the right.' And so on.

It was a nasty sensation, but sure enough, after a quarter of an hour we found the piste, although most of the stones had disappeared.

By the time we reached Merzuga, the wind had dropped as suddenly as it had risen. It remained calm until the late afternoon, when it started again. By this time we were nearly home, having taken another piste via Rissani. The sandstorm had left its mark. Twice we got stuck and had to be dug out. Fortunately for us, a group of Australians, who were camping with Jeeps, had all the necessary equipment. Without them we should probably have had to sleep in the car. This exciting and unexpected adventure added to my companions' enjoyment. They did not realize that, owing to the sad masking of the sun, the incredible beauty of colour – black desert, pink sand dunes and turquoise-blue sky – was a mere shadow of what it should have been.

Count Brando Brandolini and his wife Christiana built a house high up on the Sidi Amar road; a strange, unsatisfactory house where they spent the summers with their four boys. The house was too grand, the garden too small, and as it was built on rock, nothing grew. The land lay between the main road and the Moorish cemetery, so to purchase more was impossible. Someone said, 'You can play tennis in the house but not even ping-pong in the garden.' The house had a magnificent view but you could enjoy it only from the dining-room and Christiana's bedroom, as the other rooms looked north over the main road. The rooms with the view looked out over the cemetery.

When they first came here, Christiana was a sweet, shy little girl with a wonderful figure, soft, appealing eyes and golden hair. She had a complex about her nose which was too long and round; it in no way matched her face or figure. I loved Christiana and we become great friends.

Brando, handsome, young, amusing, generous and kind, was a complete extrovert; whereas Christiana, at that time, was an introvert. Everyone adored the beautiful, glamorous Brando, but rather ignored the shy little wife. They would entertain charmingly at their house, and we would go for picnics and long trips to the south. Little by little Christiana became more sure of herself and developed a gaiety and flirtatiousness that completely altered her character. Later on she had her nose altered, and only then did one realize what a handicap it had been, for overnight she blossomed into a beauty. From then on she became totally extrovert and was the gayest and most enchanting companion.

Eventually, as the boys got older, they sold their house here and now live at Vistorta, the family home about sixty miles from Venice. In the summer they use the Palazzo Brandolini on the Grand Canal.

Year before last I visited them at Vistorta. Christiana was away, but Brando was the same welcoming person he has always been – a little older with greying hair, but still unbelievably good-looking. The four boys, whom I had not seen for many years, were there too. They are now great strapping men and altogether a credit to Christiana and Brando. Good mannered, unspoilt and and intelligent, they seem to know what they want and are in no way influenced by the hippie movement. Brando has made Vistorta beautiful. He has created artificial lakes, planted woods, built conservatories, made waterfalls; in fact he has added all the romantic things that were missing when I went there twenty years ago.

Christiana, being born Agnelli, is a member of one of the richest families in Italy, so she was able to help Brando in beautifying Vistorta. She once told me that, in her father's will, the daughters were expected to live on their income. Times have changed since then, and she was worried at how to continue living in the way they had been accustomed.

I said, 'How difficult for you. What are you going to do to cut down?'

She answered with a sigh, 'I suppose the children won't have such expensive Christmas and birthday presents any more.'

Another time she told me that when she was driving with her brother Gianni in Turin, she noticed a splendid new hospital obviously recently finished.

'Darling, what a wonderful building. It's enormous and so much needed in Turin. Who built it?'

'You, darling,' Gianni replied.

Francis Bacon, the brilliant painter of grotesque subjects and objects, lived here for many months. This was before he became famous. He was working hard to finish a collection to be shown in

New York, and was excited at the prospect of having his first exhibition in the United States. For years his great friend had been Peter Lacey. While Francis was painting here, Peter played the piano at Dean's Bar, where he was inadequately paid, but in those days every little bit helped. Periodically Peter got very drunk and on one of his benders he took a knife and slashed three-quarters of the paintings that Francis had been working on the previous six months. Francis took it quite calmly; in fact he seemed almost pleased.

Bryce Nairn, our Consul-General at this time, was worried because Francis was frequently found by the police beaten up in some street in Tangier in the early hours of the morning. Bryce complained to the Chief of Police and asked him to have more police on duty in the darker alleys of the town. A few weeks passed; the beatings continued. Then the Chief called on Bryce and said, 'Pardon, Monsieur le Consul-General, mais il n'y a rien à faire. Monsieur Bacon aime ça.'

Brian Howard came into my life when I was about sixteen years old. He was visiting Edith Olivier, the authoress cousin of Sir Laurence Olivier. She lived in the Park at Wilton in the old dairy named the Daye House, which had been built by the Russian Lady Pembroke. Edith's father had been private chaplain to my grandfather, so my parents had given the house to her for life. Brian was young and good-looking and his mother Lura, an old friend of Edith's, rightly believed that Daye House was a good influence on Brian compared with his London life.

Brian was one of the leading figures of a set in the twenties known as the 'Bright Young People', whose main idea was to shock conventional society. The gossip columns were always relating stories of some party given by a member of this set, where Brian was always present. These parties were scandalous and ended up more often in fights, usually with the police stepping in to take over and clean up the mess. One disastrous evening ended up with Elvira Barney shooting her lover as he ran out of the house. A third cousin of mine, Elizabeth Ponsonby, was one of the leaders of this group; she was also an alcoholic. When the police arrived at the mews house, it was empty – all the guests had fled. They searched the house and eventually found Elizabeth asleep under the buffet. They had a hard time waking her. When she came to her senses they asked her if she remembered what had happened. Could she tell them who the people were who had been at the party? Had she heard the shot fired? Elizabeth, who was still muzzy, replied, 'I'm sorry, officer, but all I heard before I passed out was the clicking of the hypodermic needles.' She then passed out again.

Elizabeth was beautiful and intelligent, but like so many of that group, the end was suicide. She gassed herself in a flat above a bookshop in the King's Road. Her first cousins, Olivia and David Plunkett Green, were also members of this set. It is strange that my old cousins, Dolly Ponsonby and Gwen Plunkett Green, who were the daughters of my Herbert great-aunt, should have produced this brood. Olivia drowned herself in a lake and David killed himself in New York.

David was six feet eight inches tall. When his marriage to Babe McGusty foundered, his grandmother, who was my great-aunt Maud, said, 'Why did the silly girl marry him? Everyone knows that giants can't.'

One time Brian came to Tangier with his German boy-friend. Wherever they went, they created a scandal. I had known Brian all my life and was worried for him as he had already been refused entry to France and turned out of Spain, and I felt sure he would be asked to leave Tangier. The climax came when the German boy-friend fired his revolver at the hero on the screen of a film showing at the Mauretania Cinema. Panic ensued, complaints to our Consulate by the authorities were made. Brian and his friend must leave.

I hurried around to Bryce Nairn, our Consul-General and a sympathetic Scotsman, and begged him to let me reason with Brian. Thus he could leave of his own accord and not be expelled from yet another country. This he agreed to do, but Brian was past helping. He was furious with me. I explained how good my intentions were and how I was only trying to help him leave with dignity, as Bryce had given him forty-eight hours respite so that he could depart quietly without scandal. Brian told me to mind my own business. I got angry. Brian said, 'Louder David, prouder David. Do I see shades of Lady Londonderry? It doesn't suit you at all.'

I gave up, said goodbye and left. Twenty-four hours later I received a telegram from Gibraltar: THANK YOU STOP THE LADY LONDONDERRYS OF THIS WORLD CAN SOMETIMES BE USEFUL.

Brian, at one time, was considered the 'white hope' of the future amongst the intellectuals. He was a poet and writer, and should have become famous. Instead he drifted along, seldom worked, and spent his life more and more with people intellectually his inferior. His biographer named her book about Brian *Portrait of a Failure* – sad but apt.

He was one of the most entertaining people I have ever met. He was witty, quick and sensitive, but he became a drunkard early in life and steadily declined until in the end he killed himself in the South of France. His mother, Lura Howard, worried herself to death about her beloved Brian. She hated his father and Brian was all the world to her. She was the manager of the family firm of Mary Chess, and as long as she lived Brian at least didn't want for money. After her death, somehow Brian was unable to touch the legacy, and in his early fifties, he died a poor and bitter man.

One morning I received a letter from a very old friend, Tallulah Bankhead. This was to tell me that her sister Eugenia was coming to Tangier for the first time and would I look after her. 'Darling,' she wrote, 'She will take a lot of looking after and wear you to death. . . .'

Eugenia Bankhead lived here on and off for many years. She arrived each time in a whirlwind of furs, feathers, jewels and drink. She would either take a house, an apartment or a suite in the best hotel. Life was one long party interspersed with a few hours' massage, lots of pep pills and practically no sleep. How she existed leading this life was hard to understand. She was never depressed or bad tempered. She could and would stay up until five or six in the morning knocking back one drink after another with very little effect. She seemed always out of breath, as though she were running to catch a train. Instead she was moving from one place to another to make sure she was not missing anything more amusing than what she was currently doing. Her energy was phenomenal; there was never a dull moment when Eugenia was around.

She had a son Billy, whom she adored. She had had four

husbands, but as she said, 'Only two really, darling, as I married the same men twice.' She was always surrounded by faithful friends, male and female, who were also her stooges. They were sure to laugh or cry at the right moment. She had endless lovers but never took any of them seriously. Her sense of humour always got the better of her.

Her last fling was with a purser working for the American Export Line. She would travel back and forth all the year around to Europe on whichever boat her purser happened to be working. I think this affair was more serious than Eugenia ever meant it to be. I only hope she was happy and he treated her well.

In the past, between husbands, her great friend was Louisa Carpenter, born Dupont. A rich, masculine woman who had no children, she adopted two, but they turned out badly. She loved Eugenia's Billy and made him her heir to the Dupont millions. He is now married with children of his own. It must have been rewarding for Eugenia to know that her beloved Billy is settled for life in such happy circumstances.

It was a mystery why Eugenia had so much success. She was by no means a beauty. One eye drooped, and she was stocky and inclined to be fat, but she had the most beautiful legs and feet that I have seen on any woman. She used to say, 'It's too bad, darling, that Tallulah inherited Mummy's beauty and talent for acting, when all I inherited was Daddy's passion for fishing.' Taking a mirror out of her bag one day she said to me, 'Darling, they don't make mirrors like they used to!'

Nevertheless, summing it all up, I would say Eugenia had just as good and interesting a life as beautiful Tallulah.

The whole world seems to pass through Tangier, but occasionally one gets unexpected visitors. I am thinking particularly of two people whom one would not connect with Tangier: Dorothy Ward and her husband Shaun Glenville, mother and father of Peter Glenville, the theatrical producer. Dorothy, the greatest 'principal boy' of the century, and Shaun, the most famous 'dame', were loved all over the British Isles. When not playing in a Christmas pantomime, they took their own company touring the provinces in a series of topical revues. They were the real theatre, and as quite a young man I would wait breathlessly at the Savoy Grill for Dorothy's entrance after some first night. Tall, glamorous, red-headed, she would sweep into the restaurant wearing a wonderful white ermine coat and a spray of cattleya orchids pinned to her bosom.

Some years ago my telephone rang. It was Dorothy. She and Shaun were at the Rif Hotel. He was to celebrate his eightieth birthday in a few days' time. I decided to give a lunch party for them. They arrived looking wonderfully young and fresh. Shaun told us amusing stories about his early theatrical days, and Dorothy, the loving wife, prompted him. She was his stooge, effacing herself entirely. We toasted Shaun with champagne. Speeches were made and songs were sung until half-past four in the afternoon, when Shaun fell quietly asleep.

It had been Shaun's day, but Dorothy, always a star, had to have her day as well, so a few nights later she invited me to dinner at the Rif Hotel. I arrived to find her dressed in a fabulous sequin-encrusted evening dress, a white fox fur cape and stunning jewels. We went in to dinner. The restaurant was full, with a group of people from the Midlands where Dorothy was born. The majority of her fans came from that part of the British Isles. I thought perhaps that was why she had put on all her finery.

In the middle of dinner the manager came to our table and said, 'Miss Ward, would you be very kind and sing us a few of your old songs. Everyone in the room knows you and loves you.'

'Oh, I couldn't possibly,' said Dorothy. 'The pianist would not know my numbers and I can't sing without at least one rehearsal.'

'Oh, please,' said the manager.

'Well, if you insist, but I warn you it will be terrible.'

Dorothy went over to the pianist and whispered a few words in his ear. He played a short introduction and Dorothy let forth. She sang for thirty-five minutes. The accompanist never faltered, and I realized then that Dorothy had been rehearsing with him the whole afternoon.

The applause was deafening and Dorothy came back to take her seat at the table saying, 'I didn't do too badly, did I, considering the pianist had never accompanied me before!'

One evening, many years ago, I was having a drink at Dean's Bar with Anthony Kimmins. He was a big name in the production side of films at that period. Gerald Hamilton, a writer, sponger and unpleasant though amusing character, the original of Christopher Isherwood's *Mr Norris Changes Trains*, was sitting on the bar-stool next to us. He was obviously eavesdropping when Anthony mentioned Alexander Korda during our conversation.

'Oh,' said Gerald Hamilton, interrupting, 'Did I hear you say you were a friend of Alexander Korda? In that case, you must know my old friend Tony Kimmins.'

'I am Anthony Kimmins,' said Anthony.

Lady Diana Manners, who married Duff Cooper, was considered the greatest beauty of the century. In fact she was still beautiful and looked twenty years younger than her age, but then she was unique – like a goddess. Not many years ago she said to me, 'Oh dear, how I wish that they would let me be a "funny old thing". I am sick of being a beauty. You know, David, that one of the things that makes me shy off religion is the idea of "Life Everlasting". Can you imagine every morning for the rest of time making up this old face. Heaven, if there is a heaven, forbid.'

Diana never cared a jot what other people thought of her, and was herself totally uncritical of other people's way of life. As a girl she was considered fast, and was certainly much ahead of her time. She was expected to make a superb, important marriage; instead, she married Duff Cooper, the man she loved. No couple could have been happier or better suited, and they worshipped each other until Duff died some thirty-six years ago.

Duff had very little money when they married. Diana was determined that he should have the political career he wanted, so she accepted the role of the Madonna in *The Miracle*, written by Peter Folmuller and produced by Max Reinhardt. Everyone knows of the world-wide success she had. She untiringly played this part, touring the United States after the successful run in New York, and then the provinces of England following the London production. This lasted on and off for many years, and Diana made a small fortune which enabled Duff to continue his career – and what a triumphant career he made, becoming as he did Minister of

Information, Minister of War, First Lord of the Admiralty and British Ambassador, first in Algiers, then in Paris. Apart from this, he was an intellectual and wrote a biography of Haig, his own autobiography, *Old Men Forget*, as well as two novels, *Operation Heartbreak* and *The Boy David*.

Diana also wrote and her trilogy, *The Rainbow Comes and Goes*, *The Light of Common Day* and *Trumpets from the Steep* are perfect representations of the last fifty years. I pick them up again and again. Each time I read them, I am equally fascinated. Like Diana, they are honest: 'No autobiography is worth a damn unless the writer tells the truth, however distasteful some of it may be.' When I was writing *Second Son* I asked her if she minded my mentioning her. She answered, 'Put in anything that you like, darling, I shan't in the least mind.' A great help and a generous gesture, I think.

When I was a schoolboy, I would gaze in rapture at this unapproachable goddess, never daring to address a word to her, although I saw her often, as her sister was my aunt Marjorie, the Marchioness of Anglesey. Not until I was in my early twenties did Diana notice me. When she did, we became staunch friends, and remained so all through the years. Whenever I returned to England, she was the first person I telephoned, and we had our tête-à-tête dinner, catching up on each other's lives.

Not so long ago someone said to her, 'Wouldn't it be wonderful if Duff suddenly walked into the room?'

'Oh horrors,' answered Diana. 'What a terrible idea, seeing me as a painted old woman – and God knows what Duff looks like now.'

Her reactions were always different from those of other people. It was the unexpected in Diana that made her such a stimulating companion.

On one of my many journeys to the south of Morocco, Diana Cooper, my cousin Kitty Farrell and I decided we would be extravagant and stay at the Gazelle D'Or, the most expensive hotel in Morocco. This extraordinary place has bungalows built in the shape of an arc splaying out each side of the main building that houses only the dining-room, sitting-rooms and bar. The Gazelle D'Or was designed and constructed by Baron Pelanque, a Belgian. It is set deep in the country and you approach it through a long drive of giant bamboos that meet overhead like the aisle of a cathedral. The hotel itself is unpretentious from the outside and painted the traditional ochre colour. The bunglows are set far apart and each is surrounded by its own garden, so that the neighbouring one is invisible. They all look on to a rough field full of wild flowers, where camels are lazily chewing the cud. Each consists of a double bedroom, bathroom, dressing-room and sitting-room; a shaded terrace looks on to the field.

As you walk through the hall and sitting-rooms of the main block, you reach the garden entrance, and your eye travels down a winding stream with a twisting path each side. It is beautifully planted with exotic flowers which fade naturally into the adjoining fields. At the end of this pastoral walk, you reach the swimming-pool, which is hidden from view by clumps of orange and lemon trees. The changing-rooms, showers and loos are built of bamboo with thatched roofs. Behind these are the tennis-courts, completely hidden. Nothing ugly is visible. To my wind, the only vulgar note is the floor of one of the sitting-rooms which is tiled in garish mosaics depicting the signs of the zodiac. Of course for tourists it is interesting, but it seems different in style from the other rooms, which have the atmosphere of a private home.

On arrival, the first thing you see are the stables with beautiful Arab horses waiting to be ridden by the rich guests, most of whom, so Jean Pelanque told me, fall off the moment they get on. They either never ride again, or persevere until they break an arm or a leg, and then blame Jean for keeping such vicious horses!

When Diana, Kitty and I arrived, I introduced them to Jean, who was delighted to meet Diana and said that we must be his guests, though, alas, he was leaving the next day. We had planned to stay three nights. The first day and night we wallowed in the luxury at Jean's expense; the following day Diana said we had better save what was left of the butter, bread and cheese and fruit from our breakfast trays. Then we could buy a bottle of wine and some salami and go somewhere for a picnic. This we did both remaining days. We ate small dinners, for the prices were astronomical. The last evening, the head-waiter came up and said, 'I have been worried because you have eaten so little. Was the food not good? Was the wine bad?'

We said, 'Oh no, but we are on a diet.'

10 Three generations of Herberts: the author with his nephew, the present Earl of Pembroke, and great-nephew William, in the garden of Wilton House, 1989.

11 Mme Schlumberger, Sheikha Fatima al-Sabah of Kuwait, and the author at York Castle, the house of M. Yves Vidal in Tangier.

12 The author with his sister (left), Viscountess Hambledon, lady-in-waiting to Queen Elizabeth the Queen Mother, and his sister-in-law, Mary Countess of Pembroke.

13 The author with Ira Belline, niece of Stravinsky, and a young actor, Shane Oneil, lunching in his garden in Tangier, 1968.

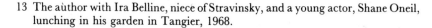

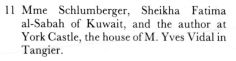

14 Left to right: the author; Princess Marina, Duchess of Kent; the author's brother, Sidney Earl of Pembroke; Princess Olga of Yugoslavia (sister of Princess Marina), in the Italian Garden at Wilton House.

15 The author with Princess Ali Khan, mother of the Aga Khan, and her husband, Lord Camrose, visiting Tangier on their honeymoon, 1987.

16 The author surrounded by the Muscle Men, a team of acrobats, at a fancy dress party in Morocco, 1988.

17 The author in his garden with Paul Bowles.

18 Alvilde Lees-Milne, the authoress and landscape gardener, with the author at
Malcolm Forbes's party, Tangier, 1989.

19 The author at eighty.

'What a pity,' he said, 'because you were invited by Monsieur le Baron for your entire visit!'

I enjoy my visits to England, but after three weeks I am ready to return to Tangier because it is home (and after a certain age, there is no place like it). The everyday chores of running a house, looking after the garden, feeding the birds, doing the marketing and working for the local charities run by the British community, keep me occupied. In England I have none of these things to occupy my time. When I see others with their busy lives, I feel frustrated and restless. The weekends spent with friends and relations are a great pleasure; it is during the week that time lies rather heavy on my hands. Each year there are fewer friends left, and so, fewer houses to visit. For example, Cecil Beaton at Reddish House and Michael Duff at Vayno have both gone within a year. One must expect this, but it is difficult to readjust oneself.

When I do go home, I spend more time staying with my sister Patricia, or my nephew Henry at Wilton, or until very recently the Droghedas at Virginia Water, than I do in London.

In October 1979 my nephew Henry Pembroke and his wife Claire gave a ball at Wilton. When Henry told me about it, I asked him what it was in aid of. He answered, 'Ourselves. The children are growing up, and it's the last chance we shall have to give a party for friends of our own age and older.'

It happened on a clear, still, autumn night. The House and the Palladian bridge floodlit were dreams of beauty; the shadows cast by the horizontal branches of the huge cedars on the smooth, velvety lawn were magical. The inside of the House was breathtakingly beautiful. The painted ceilings in the state rooms were invisibly lit from behind the cornices, and the Kent and Chippendale gilt furniture, covered in crimson velvet of the same date, glowed with a rich warmth. The Wyatt Cloisters, built around the quadrangle, were banked with flowers. Here supper was served at round tables seating eight people. Each table was lit by candles.

We danced in the Double Cube Room with its ten Vandykes, seven of which are full length family portraits; the other three are of King Charles, his wife Henrietta Maria, and the conversation painting of their three children which hangs over the mantelpiece.

It was fascinating remembering the changing fashion of dress for the women during the years. The men, on the other hand, remained the same – white ties and tail coats, until the last occasion, when dinner-jackets were worn. The women had not had much chance of wearing their tiaras these past years, so the excitement was great when the invitations read: *Tiaras will be worn.* Those who owned them got them out of the bank; those who didn't, borrowed or hired them. For me it was sad, for the hair-styles of today are not designed to carry tiaras, nor are the so-called evening dresses compatible with them. In fact, some of the women resembled the ugly sisters in a Cinderella pantomime.

At the west end of the Double Cube Room below Vandyke's huge picture of the Pembroke family of the day, there is a banquette about twenty feet long. In the old days nervous débutantes used to sit there waiting for some eligible young man to ask them to dance. The pretty ones were snapped up immediately, while the plain ones sat uncomfortably with an expectant look on their faces. At this last party the banquette was given over to the older guests – Cecil Beaton and Michael Duff amongst them. It was a strange feeling to look at that row of elderly faces and remember that so many of them were in their teens at the first ball my mother and father gave for my sister Patricia's coming-out. Years later my parents gave another ball for my elder brother's coming of age.

Many years passed. The 1939–45 war started and Wilton was requisitioned, becoming Southern Command headquarters for the duration and several years afterwards. When the Army left, there was found to be dry rot in the woodwork of the Double and Single Cube Rooms, and the House was under scaffolding for a long period. When the work was finished, the House and gardens were opened to the public. My mother, who enjoyed organizing, threw herself heart and soul into the project. Guides were recruited and taught the history of the House, the family, pictures and furniture. She opened a successful restaurant in the Stables, at which she served herself. The venture proved successful and was a great help in keeping Wilton going, but the way of life for my parents was, naturally, not the same as before the war. Everything was on a much diminished scale. Weekend parties were fewer, so were the guests. Many bedrooms were closed; they lived in the library, my father's study and my mother's sitting-room. A large part of the garden away from the house was left untended, but the beauty of Wilton was such that nothing could take away its quality of peace and serenity.

When my father died in the sixties, my brother Sidney succeeded. As my father had made everything over to him at his coming of age, the finances were in much better shape. He and my sister-in-law Mary set to work to redecorate the rooms which had been unused all those years. He had the pictures cleaned, rehung and relit, and the furniture repaired. He had great knowledge. Experts came down many times to view the treasures. Many pictures were found to be of great value. Before, they had been unidentified.

Sidney gave his eldest daughter, my niece Diane Herbert, a dance when she was eighteen. A few years later he gave another for his son Henry's twenty-first birthday, so at the age of seventy-two I have witnessed five of these splendid entertainments.

PART FOUR

I imagine that in the minds of some people my life here consists of doing nothing. Maybe that's true, but I seem to be constantly busy. Days fly by without my having enough time to do all the things I want to do. The social life is not all-important, as it was in the days when Tangier was international, but it still plays a large part in my everyday life. In this chapter I shall try to describe the international days, Tangier now, and the people who still make it an interesting place in which to live.

Tangier is not a place in which to do nothing unless you are getting old. Then it is ideal. You can sit in the street cafés and watch the pageant go by, a mixture of many nationalities in various forms of fancy dress, from the dignified Moroccan men in white djellabas to veiled ladies, American and English hippies, Spanish whores, merchant seamen of every country, dapper Moroccan officers and sailors, sailors from visiting fleets of France, Holland, England, America and Spain, shoeshine boys, pimps, guides, tourist groups, flower vendors and water-carriers – an unending stream of fascinating individuals. Sometimes, after an hour or so, I become as giddy as I do when watching tennis at Wimbledon.

I had been visiting Tangier and the interior of Morocco for many years before I came to live here permanently. In those days, Tangier was an International Zone; the northern half of Morocco was Spanish, and the southern half a French Protectorate. Europeans controlled the country to such an extent that one rarely met Moroccans, except the grandest of families or those chosen by the various powers in charge. It was extremely difficult to get to know the people of Morocco – not one's servants, of course, or waiters, taxi-drivers or shopkeepers, all of whom were polite, friendly and eager to please, but Moroccans who shared the same interests as myself. It took me many years before I could say that I had made real friends amongst them and appreciated their warmth and innate good manners.

There were one or two important families whom we met. Chief of those were the Menebhis. They were clever, intelligent people who took no part in the running of Tangier. Menebhi's father was Minister of War during the reign of Abdel Aziz and was knighted by Edward VII when Harry Maclean was made a Caid by the Sultan. Maclean had come to Morocco to instruct the army in modern warfare. Other Moroccans we saw occasionally at official gatherings. Then it was only the men we met; the wives never appeared, even at lunch, tea or dinner in their own homes, if there was a man not belonging to the family present. With few exceptions, Tangier society at that time consisted of a collection of petty officials of all nationalities augmented by respectable gangsters, smugglers and a few crooked bankers. They lived cheek by jowl with the Committee of Control, the Administrator and the numerous representatives of the twenty-odd legations. It was a completely false atmosphere but hilariously funny if you did not take it seriously. Most of these people were immensely grand, battling for the best seats at functions, offended and insulted if wrongly placed at luncheons or dinners. At the time of Independence, they all ran like rabbits. I often wonder to what semi-detached villas they returned.

Tangier remained static for many years after Independence and did not progress. It did not collapse, but they were lean years. However, Tangier has always been the gateway of Morocco and thinks itself such. One must remember, too, that Tangier is not the real Morocco; it has changed hands so often over the centuries. Its inhabitants are different in many ways from the Moroccans in other parts of the country. Tangier people refer to those as foreigners or tourists. Equally, the rest of Morocco looks upon Tangier as something different.

I am pleased that recently a great effort is being made to re-establish Tangier to its rightful place in the Kingdom of Morocco. Plans are going forth for the development of the Bay of Tangier into a holiday and entertainment spot for tourists, including hotel complexes, holiday homes, casinos, night-clubs and a marina. There is also a tunnel or bridge project under serious discussion which would connect Morocco and Spain, linking Europe and Africa over or under the Strait of Gibraltar. The King's mother has bought an old house situated close to my own and rebuilt it in traditional Moroccan style. She spends most of the summer here. The King's eldest sister, Princess Lalla Aicha, who was Ambassador to the Court of St James's some years ago, frequently spends summer months at her beach house at Restinga. I am sure if all goes to plan, in a few years' time we shall not recognize our almost defeated Tangier.

Each summer more visitors arrive to spend their holidays in Tangier. I don't mean groups, but private individuals who rent villas and apartments. If you wish to spend July and August in Tangier, it is essential to make your plans a year ahead. Every summer, as usual, there is an influx of new people: the designers Valentino, Yuki and Roger Vivier; the actors Robert Hirsh and Raymond Gerome; the artist Claudio Bravo, who has built a house on the Marshan; Fabrice Emaier, creator of the Palace in Paris; Prince and Princess Lubkowitz; Christopher Gibbs and Dewi Sukarno, to name but a few. Also many Italian friends of Lalla Aicha, the King's sister, made during her years as Ambassador in Rome. Adolfo de Velasco used to rent two bungalows at Robinson's Plage, a lovely motel on the Atlantic. He gave lunch every day to almost anyone who dropped in. Sometimes up to thirty people descended on him, some saying 'just for a drink' but invariably staying to lunch. He is the perfect host, welcoming and generous to a fault.

As well as European visitors, Moroccans from all over the country spend their holidays in Tangier. Hardly an evening passes without a dinner party or a dance. At one of my parties, there were no fewer than sixteen different nationalities present: Moroccan, British, French, American, Italian, Spanish, Hungarian, Belgian, Swiss, Polish, Peruvian, Argentinian, Tunisian, Greek, Dutch and German. The total number of guests was only twenty-eight.

Tangier still has an international flavour and has never quite lost its happy-go-lucky atmosphere. Fun though the summer is, one does give a sigh of relief when September comes and we go back to our quiet village life.

York Castle, the most beautiful house in the Casbah, is now owned by Yves Vidal, a Frenchman who until a few years ago was European director of Knoll International. He now works in public relations, dividing his time between France, the United States and Morocco. York Castle was originally the Governor's House in the time of King Charles II, whose wife Catherine of Braganza brought Tangier, as well as Bombay, to the British throne as part of her dowry. Over the years York Castle fell into ruins, being bought eventually by the Marquess of Bute in the early part of this century. He restored it and gave it to his third son, Lord Rhidian Crichton Stuart, who lived there with his Dutch wife and family for many years. When the children grew up, they returned to England and sold York Castle. The buyer, a Mr Tower, was not allowed by the authorities to live in Tangier. He said he was retired, but they discovered he had been in the Secret Service in various parts of the Arab world and was still employed by the British Government. Yves had always loved York Castle and wanted to buy it. I told him that I would keep my ears and eyes open and wire him if it ever came on the market. Our Consul-General here made inquiries in Rabat and was told that Mr Tower was *persona non grata*. I at once sent a telegram to Yves and within a short time he was the owner.

Many years had elapsed since the Crichton Stuarts finally left, so the house was in a state of dilapidation. Yves, Robert Gerofi, a Belgian architect, and Charles Sevigny, a brilliant decorator, set to work and restored it to its former beauty. York Castle has been publicized in all the art magazines. Each July Yves gives one memorable party which continues until dawn, Moroccan musicians alternating with European. Everybody dances in the vast patio around a mosaic pool; many seem to end up in the pool, whether they like it or not. Friends of Yves come over from the Costa del Sol, and York Castle is full of friends from Paris.

Yves also arranged an Arabian Nights evening in aid of the Petits Lits Blancs and our local charities. It was an unforgettable occasion. The Casbah was transformed; the Place de la Casbah was covered with beautiful carpets from all over Morocco. A huge tent housed the bar, making it invisible from the outside. The ramparts were lined with soldiers dressed in the uniforms of the time of the Sultan Moulay Ismael. Banners of different colours and designs attached to long poles waved gently in the breeze. Electricity was forbidden, so this magical scene was lit only by flaming torches. Donkeys, horses and camels wondered amidst the guests. One side of the Casbah is on a different level from the main square, and on this dais dancers from all over Morocco sat in circles, each group forming different patterns, the women dressed in filmy gauze garments glittering with paillettes and sparkling with jewels, resembling bunches of wild flowers. The men, for the most part, were dressed in white with turbans or the local headdress worn from whatever part of Morocco they came. The effect was miraculous; lying on the steps outside the Sultan's Palace, one felt as though a Delacroix had come to life.

Supper was served inside the palace and the adjoining gardens – again no electric lights were allowed to take away the atmosphere of bygone days and candles and torches were the sole illuminations. It was an evening of sheer visual delight and something I shall remember all my life.

Last summer Yves Vidal gave a party on 14 July, which is France's national day. In contrast to the celebrations marking the French Revolution, which were held in Paris and all the other big cities, Yves's party was to remember all those who died on the guillotine during the Reign of Terror that followed. We were told to come dressed in white, and the entrance hall was draped with material on which was printed the fleur-de-lis. It was a charming and touching evening. Two orchestras played till the early hours of the morning and a wonderful singer, the new Edith Piaf, entertained us with songs from the sixties and seventies in her strange, strident voice.

There were many other parties given during the summer, but the climax was, without doubt, Malcolm Forbes's seventieth birthday extravaganza. To be honest, it was difficult to understand what it was all about, as three-quarters of the guests had never met Malcolm. It was more a giant publicity stunt than a birthday party. This did not take away from the fact that it was a glorious spectacle. The Marshan, which is a large open square, was strewn with beautiful rugs and carpets, and the King's splendid horses, their riders dressed in traditional Moorish costumes, were lined up to welcome the guests. Groups of exquisitely robed dancers and singers had been brought in from every corner of Morocco: they danced and sang to their fascinating tribal music, as we arrived at the Forbes house, named the Old Mendoubia. The entrance to the house is narrow and we were forced to stand in line for too long before entering the hall. Once past this obstacle we were asked to put our hands in a sort of bran dip and pull out a ticket, which showed us in which tent we were to sit. Having survived these formalities, we walked through into the garden. It was truly a lovely sight. Six enormous Moroccan tents were pitched on the grass, beautifully decorated and becomingly lit with exquisite bouquets of flowers placed on every table. Each tent was labelled – The Gold Tent, The Red Tent, the Blue Tent, and so on.

Alvilde Lees-Milne and her daughter Clarissa were staying with me, and Malcolm had kindly included them in my invitation. After a struggle we found our tent, which happened to be the gold one. It was the tent presided over by the eldest Forbes son. Many friends of mine were in this tent, including the Anders, Drue Heinz, Christopher Gibbs and Adolfo de Velasco. On arrival we were asked if we would separate and each of us go to three different tables where fifteen American guests were already seated. As we knew none of them we were at first rather put out, but, as it happened, they were delightful people and we enjoyed a very jolly dinner. Later on, comparing notes with my house guests, we discovered that not one of the forty-two people at our respective tables had ever seen, let alone met our host. They were all in some measure associated in a business way with the Forbes empire.

Elizabeth Taylor was the guest of honour, the Crown Prince of Morocco and his brother were present, as was Angus Ogilvy, the Henry Kissingers and many other famous people. The birthday cake was, I imagine, the largest ever made – four tiers standing on six-foot columns. It was transported to the party on a vast lorry and by a miracle arrived unscathed. There were nearly a thousand guests, so I suppose if the cake had been smaller there would not have been enough to go around.

Malcolm made a delightful speech, short and to the point. He really was a thoroughly nice character, unpretentious, kind and humorous – quite different from his public image.

A rich American couple were lent a beautiful castle in the Casbah. Most of their guests were equally rich. I was asked to dinner and the host, looking round the room, said to me, 'Which of the couples in this room would you say had the least money?'

I said, 'All the women have lovely jewellery, and all look beautifully dressed. It's difficult to answer.'

'Go on,' he said. 'Guess.'

There happened to be only one couple whom I liked, so I chose them.

'Gosh,' he said. 'You're right. They've only got $20,000 a day!'

The hostess drank a lot, and one evening after dinner as she was sitting on a revolving chair, she started going round and round, laughing like a maniac. She went round once too many times and the seat came out of its socket, whereupon the lady was catapulted half-way across the room, landing with terrific force on the tiled floor. She broke her wrist and badly bruised her face. It was difficult not to laugh, but it ruined her holiday. They never returned.

I entertained them in my house several times for the sake of an old friend who owns the castle. The day before they left, they asked me to come and say goodbye, as they wished to give me a present. It consisted of all the half-empty bottles of drink they had not consumed.

Tangier was a disastrous town for people of weak character. Life was so easy and so cheap in the international period. Drinks were for nothing, bars never closed and the police were indulgent, to say the least. During the time I have lived here, several people I have known have drunk themselves to death. Tangier is no longer cheap; the Administration is strict, so the easy-going atmosphere of the old days has disappeared. Yet I have some acquaintances who still live their lives on bar-stools. Only recently I heard someone say, 'Oh, how I long for the nights! The days are so difficult to get through.'

One evening I was sitting with friends at a table in the corner of a well-known night-club when a weedy, nondescript looking young man wandered in and sat down at the bar. At almost the same moment a middle-aged man a few tables away from us banged his glass down on the table with a terrible crash. Everybody stopped talking. 'You – get off that bar-stool,' the man said.

The one at the bar turned his head slowly round and met the

eyes of the other man. I have seldom seen such an expression of abject terror.

'Get on your knees,' the voice continued. 'Now crawl on your belly to my table.'

As though hypnotized, the wretched creature commenced to wriggle across the floor. When he reached the table, white and shivering, the voice said, 'I should kill you, but I won't. There are too many witnesses here.' And with that he smashed his beer glass on the young man's head and kicked him full on the mouth.

There was a terrible scream of pain; blood and teeth covered the floor. Then the wretch fainted. None of us moved except the gangster who stood up, bowed to us all, smiled and said 'Goodnight', then walked slowly out of the place.

We were all stunned and demanded an explanation from the owners. It appeared that the middle-aged man was an important gangster in the London underworld. The youth had been a member of his gang, but recently had turned Queen's Evidence, which had forced the gangster to flee to Tangier.

We left the bar shaken, and never went back.

Every summer, usually in the month of August, a Spaniard arrives to stay at the Minzah Hotel. He is a bachelor with what he calls 'my two boys'. They are monkeys: one large with a white chest and immensely long arms, the other small and golden with an unusually long tail. They are dressed in beautifully cut clothes which are changed twice during the day. They are clean and well behaved. Each morning they are washed, brushed and combed before coming down to the garden and the swimming-pool where they swing from the trees and turn somersaults. In every way they resemble high-spirited children. Children are at first nervous of them, but I have seen the black monkey run up to a little girl, take her by the hand and drag her off to have a game of catch. Once the ice is broken, they play happily together. The Spaniard told me how easy it was to train them if you acquire them when they are a few days old. 'My two boys are now three years old, sophisticated, intelligent and have beautiful manners. I can take them anywhere without having to worry about their behaviour. The other day they went to a tea party at Louise de Meuron's and sat in their chairs eating cakes and drinking tea like two well-brought-up young gentlemen.'

I asked him about sleeping arrangements and he said, 'They sleep side by side in a small bed next to mine, and like all children when the lights are turned out, they are instantly asleep and don't move till the morning.'

I inquired about scratching. 'What?' he said, looking very hurt, 'I've told you that they have their bath every morning.'

My own monkey was a rhesus. His testicles and bottom were azure blue, his fur was like chinchilla, his golden eyes were mean and he hated me. When I first saw Punkey, he was sitting on a juke-box in a night-club. He had been bought by a Moroccan from an English sailor off a visiting yacht. The owner of the vessel refused to keep Punkey on board. I stayed at the night-club till five in the morning haggling with the new owner. Eventually he gave in, and Punkey drove home with me, holding my hand. He slept in a bookcase by my bed and I thought that he was my friend for life. He was very young, but perhaps not young enough, for after two years he bit me to the bone. For many years he lived in a large cage in the garden and made a horrible face at me whenever I passed by. He died peacefully a few years ago.

James Wyllie died in his late eighties. He lived in Tangier for fifty years or more. His house in the Casbah was a sheer delight, and in the patio you sat and ate delicious meals under what Jim loved to tell you was the same fig tree under which Pepys wrote his Tangier Diary. Jim was always gay, welcoming and full of amusing anecdotes. Sometimes people feel nervous about remaining in Morocco, as when the unsuccessful attempts on the King's life happened in recent years. Jim always said, 'Nonsense. I've been told I'd better leave at least every five years for the last fifty, and here I still am.' He painted excellent water-colours, chiefly of the Moroccan landscape in the Atlas or further south, and had several successful exhibitions in London and Tangier.

Jim used to spend his winters with a great friend and well-known archaeologist, Bar Richmond Brown, who died before Jim. His death was a blow to Jim who was many years his senior, but I often feel that it gives older people an extra zest when someone much younger dies. By this I do not mean that Jim was heartless or that he did not miss his friend a great deal; it is simply a theory I have. I well remember my father looking every morning at the deaths and births in *The Times* and saying to my mother, 'Good God, old so and so is dead – years younger than me, you know', and smiling contentedly.

Tangier was a comparatively small town, but though it is growing at a rapid pace, people are still apt to think of it as isolated. This is untrue, as you can fly direct from here to London, Paris, Madrid, Lisbon, Geneva, Brussels and Amsterdam. There is a twice-daily flight to Gibraltar – a vast improvement since the days when a daily flight to Gibraltar and a twice-weekly flight to Madrid was all that we could boast of.

Tourists arriving for the first time are surprised at how green the countryside is surrounding the airport. They expect Africa to be scorched earth, instead of which they see fields of wild flowers and orchards of fig, almond and cherry trees as they drive to Tangier through unspoilt country over a road lined with eucalyptus trees. I have travelled three-quarters of the world but have yet to find anywhere comparable. Tangier itself is not a beautiful city by any standards, but its position is unique. Built on many small hills and two larger ones, it dominates the Strait of Gibraltar where the Atlantic and Mediterranean meet. Even on the calmest day these two seas fight and it is rough. This is why we have such a variety of fish – fish from both seas.

The views are splendid. You see Gibraltar, the coast of southern Spain from Algeciras to Trafalgar, the North African coast from Tangier to Ceuta, and Morocco's range of the Rif Mountains with lush, undulating country below them. To add to the beauty of these surroundings, Tangier has extraordinary light. It is difficult to describe, but the only other country I have visited that has the same clarity and glow is Greece.

The beaches around Tangier are beautiful. There is nothing more restful than spending the day on one of them if you are nervous or overtired. When you think how close we are to Europe, where every beach is packed with people all summer long, we are truly lucky. Even in August, the height of the tourist season, the beaches, apart from the town beach which is always crowded, are for the most part deserted. You can drive thirty miles or more south through unspoilt country by the edge of the sea where the sand is golden, clean and free of pollution. You rarely meet anyone, and if you do, it is a Moroccan on horseback riding into the sea to cool off in the summer heat, a shepherd leading his flock, or a few cows standing in the shallows refreshing their hot feet. It is like going back a thousand years; small groups of people clothed in their national dress riding their donkeys along the sand resemble figures out of the Bible.

When I was younger, a party of friends and I walked from the Grottes d'Hercule to Asilah, a town eighteen miles further along the Atlantic coast. We left early in the morning with a picnic lunch. We swam every two miles or so, slept after lunch, and arrived late in the afternoon.

Asilah is a fishing village built on high rock by the edge of the sea. The houses are painted white or pale blue and the town is surrounded by walls built by the Portuguese in the eighteenth century. It is as unspoilt today as it must have been then. There are several fish restaurants, and whilst eating your lunch you can watch the fishermen bringing in their catch, a wonderful assort-ment of fish – lobsters, crabs, sole, plaice, shrimps, sardines, anchovies, clams and squid. They are hardly out of the sea before they are cooked and eaten. You pick and choose what you like best from the several plates of different fish put on the table all at once. In the summer this is an ideal way of lunching as it doesn't last too long. After you have eaten, you can walk a hundred yards down to the sea where you can sleep off your lunch before plunging into the water again. When I take my friends there after only two and a half hours' flying from London, they say, 'We feel we are in paradise.'

During the occupation of northern Morocco by the Spaniards, the Governor and Commander-in-Chief's headquarters was in the town of Tetuan. He lived in a beautiful Moorish palace in a romantic garden overlooking the main square. In the same town a lovely titian-haired Englishwoman had rented a villa for health reasons. She was tubercular and lived the life of a semi-invalid; but this did not prevent her from catching the eye of the Governor. She became his mistress and was for many years 'the power behind the throne'. She was nicknamed 'The Dubarry of Tetuan' and was a great help to us all.

Crossing the frontier from the International Zone to the Spanish Zone was a nightmare. It took at least two hours before you were allowed to pass, for the Customs officers searched each and every suitcase, parcel, handbag and wallet. They would then pull the car apart and, not content with that, they stripped one naked in some small cubicle. They were rude, dirty and totally uncivilized. If you were a friend of 'The Dubarry' and wished to go to the Spanish Zone, all you had to do was ring her up and say when you were coming. She then sent you a small sheet of the Governor's writing-paper with her name written on it. When this was produced at the frontier, all the mean, lazy Customs officers and policemen sprang to attention and waved you through.

Later 'The Dubarry' moved to a much grander house and her old mother, who came to visit her, said, 'Isn't my little daughter clever to manage so well on such a small income?'

We were all fond of 'The Dubarry' and were sad for her when the Governor was recalled to Madrid. She genuinely loved him and felt sure she would lose him in a great city like Madrid with so many beautiful women.

One day she came to Tangier and was in despair. How should she dress? What sort of jewellery should she wear? How could she keep him in love with her? Shura de Muntz, a Polish woman, had a dress shop in the Minzah Hotel. I took 'The Dubarry' to see her and we discussed clothes for hours. Eventually both Shura and I decided she must wear black only; for in black, with her titian hair and wonderful English complexion, she could hold her own any-where. She had not been a good dresser and she had never worn black. She thought we were mad, but after a great deal of flattery and cajolery, we convinced her. Shura designed her trousseau and 'The Dubarry' then left for Madrid.

We were right. She kept her lover until the war broke out, at which she left for Portugal and I believe opened a night-club. When I last heard of her, she was living on the coast of southern Spain.

A certain woman living here had no passport; she came from a country behind the Iron Curtain. Naturally she wished to have some form of legal papers. She had a fair amount of money but not much physical charm. A dominant woman, she decided to become a British citizen. She met every passenger liner coming from the United Kingdom, and in those days there were many of them. It was also the time when the English were very restricted in the amount of money they could take out of Great Britain, so they were always short of cash. She would stand on the quay and watch the passengers descend. She was interested only in the single men. She realized that she did not have much hope with the normal ones, so she did not waste her time with them; any likely looking homo-sexual was her quarry. She would sidle up to one of them, get into conversation and say, 'I expect you are short of money. I will give you £100 if you will marry me – no strings attached. You see, I am stateless and need a passport. After the ceremony you need never see me again. You will be perfectly free and I will have my passport.'

It is a sad story because it did not work. No one would take up the offer. She persevered just too long, for one day two men, unknown to each other, went to complain to our Consul-General. He summoned her to his office and told her that if she did this once more, he would be forced to tell the authorities that she had no papers and was here under false pretences.

Somehow she did get married, but not to an Englishman. She lived here until recently as an extremely successful business woman. Where she is now I have no idea.

Today many people use the word 'eccentric' wrongly. Here in Tangier it applies to somebody who takes drugs, drinks and leads a thoroughly sordid life. This is not the real meaning of the word, but I fear, with so few real eccentrics left, it will become so.

Michael Scott is an eccentric, but lives here so little of the year that I cannot count him as a true resident. His wife, Cherry, who worked for the Save the Children Society before she married, has a house in Cambridge and comes here rarely. They have twin daughters, Sarah and Caroline, who keep Cherry busy, but Michael is a wanderer. Cherry never knows where he is, where he is going or where he has been. He has adopted and discarded many religions and cults, but returns to Christianity after short lapses.

When he is in Tangier he disappears for days on end, probably to attend some meeting of a local saint. On one occasion when he was away, his home and garden were invaded by a horde of hippies who had suddenly found Christ. The place was in a shambles. The authorities became aware of this state of affairs because it was discovered that these newly recruited Christians were proselytizing amongst the local Muslim boys.

I telephoned Cambridge and spoke to Cherry. I said, 'Michael must come out immediately or perhaps the house will be confiscated.'

'Of course, I'll try and find him and send him out at once.'

He came by bus from England, taking six days! When he did arrive, after a great deal of persuasion he grudgingly turned the hippies out.

Michael is a fascinating personality, erudite and humorous, with a beautiful speaking voice. He can enthral you with his stories. He is not quite of this world. His feet are several yards off the ground and he seldom comes down to earth. His house is an enchanting mess. He and Cherry are true Bohemians and total chaos reigns. Time does not exist for them. I love them both, and enjoy to the full their late luncheon parties on rickety chairs under a pear tree.

I was invited to an official dinner party at the Minzah Hotel to meet the members of a conference that was taking place in Tangier. The delegates were multicoloured, and I was placed next to a tall, handsome, black gentleman. We conversed in French during the meal. This was unnecessary, as I discovered towards the end of the dinner that he spoke perfect English. I was interested to find out what his job was, so I said, 'I hope you don't think it impertinent, but what is your job?' 'I'm a king actually,' he replied.

At another function of the same sort I was seated next to the younger brother of a potentate from the Middle East. We were watching a dance competition of jiving and rock and roll. The dancers were of all nationalities and doing their utmost to win the first prize. The competition was finally won by a French girl and her partner, a Spanish boy. When this was announced, the young prince turned to me and said, 'Isn't it strange that although all the movements and rhythms come from my part of the world, the Occidentals manage to dance a great deal better than the Orientals?'

New people are coming to settle in Tangier and become residents of Morocco. Many are interesting and intelligent. Noel Mostert, a writer who recently had an overwhelming success with *Supership*, his book on giant tankers, is one of them. Before this book, Noel had written articles and short stories for the *Reader's Digest*, *The New Yorker* and other important magazines, but he never dreamed that this book would bring him immediate fame.

Noel is a strange character. Born in South Africa, a godson of General Smuts, he left his homeland and became a Canadian subject to register his disapproval of apartheid. He was always at loggerheads with his father. They were totally unsympathetic, one to the other. He loved his mother, but she, as was only right, stuck by her husband in all disputes. Noel's father is now dead and his mother has been got hold of by a religious group who little by little are eating up what should be Noel's inheritance.

Noel is difficult to understand. For no apparent reason he will take offence, but when he is in good spirits he is a delightful companion and full of humour. He is a worrier and never sure of what he wants to do. He also asks your advice, you give it and he will invariably go straight to someone else, ask that person's advice, and take neither.

We met by accident on a tender leaving a P&O liner at Gibraltar. We had done the trip from England together but had not got acquainted on the voyage. On the tender at 5 a.m. in the dark we found ourselves sitting next to each other. We rocked about for several hours; our faces were practically invisible as the tender was so badly lit. Eventually the sun rose and each saw what the other looked like. By this time we had become friends, having carried on an animated conversation to pass the time. We spent the day together in Gibraltar, and in the evening I flew back to Tangier and Noel took the ferry to Algeciras.

A long time passed before we met again. I happened to walk into a bar called the Carousel and there was Noel. I said, 'Why didn't you ring me?'

'Oh, I didn't think you'd remember me.'

'Nonsense,' I said. 'I shall never forget those dark hours in the cold early morning as long as I live.'

This is typical of Noel's strange personality. His diffidence is inapposite, as he is much appreciated and admired by all who know him. Perhaps the success of *Supership* will change him and give him more self-confidence. I am an extrovert; Noel is an introvert, so perhaps my criticism is unjustified. I am devoted to Noel, and would love to give him some of my overdeveloped self-confidence.

Another newcomer is Anne Lambton, also a writer. She was married to my cousin, Teddy Lambton, the trainer. They parted company some years ago, and Anne went to Beirut where she lived for several years. She arrived here on a visit with Lebanese friends. They rented an apartment. The friends moved on, Anne stayed. She has now bought a house and has decided to live here permanently. She was sad to leave Beirut and her circle of friends, but with the political situation as it was, it would have been madness for her to return. For many years she has been a newspaper reporter and written various articles, chiefly on fashion. She is tall, willowy and smiling. Her blonde hair is cut in Joan of Arc style, she moves with elegance and, though not strictly beautiful, she has great allure, being always beautifully dressed.

Anne's first novel, *The Sisters*, was published in America. The background of the picture on the dust-jacket depicts the White House with two girls in profile in the foreground, so it is anybody's guess who they are. The novel, she admits, was written primarily to earn money, as she is not well off. Although well written, it is crude and sexy – what the public wants. I was so startled at some of the passages that I had to reread them to be sure that my imagination had not run away with me. In spite of this, the story carries you along at terrific speed and the characters, odious as they are, fascinate you to such an extent that you become angry and would like to exterminate the lot. It was fairly successful and makes Anne a certain amount of money. She has written two more novels and a book on horse-breeding. Now she gives exhibitions in London and New York of her needlework pictures of cats.

To the outside world Anne gives the impression of being a rather hard, self-assured, career woman, but I have detected a sad, worried look in her eyes from time to time. I do not know her well enough yet to ask her if I am right, but I am sure the real Anne is not the one she wishes us all to see.

Yet another author, Gavin Lambert, has come to settle in Tangier, which seems to be becoming the 'Writers' Paradise'. Gavin made his name in Hollywood as a scriptwriter, and since then has written several powerful books, including *The Slide Area*. He is a quiet, self-effacing person whose work is all-important to him. He writes during the day and emerges in the evening with such beautiful manners that, at first, you feel he is sedate. He creates a gentle, old-fashioned atmosphere, but then suddenly he glitters. He is astringent, witty, quizzical, and his lively eyes miss nothing. He has a solemn expression which makes his explosive laughter irresistible.

Gavin is an intellectual in the true sense. By that I mean he mixes with people of all sorts and never makes them feel inferior or ignorant. No one enjoys a stimulating talk more than Gavin.

Lesley Blanch, author of *The Wilder Shores of Love*, *Sabres of Paradise*, *Journey into the Mind's Eye*, *Pavilion of Love* and many others, is a beloved friend of Gavin. I met her for the first time last year when she came to stay with him. This was a privilege. Her appearance is fascinating and marries perfectly with her books – fair-haired, blue eyed, pink and white complexion. Her strange oriental way of dressing enhances her English rose quality. Though exotic in appearance, she is down to earth conversationally. She is offended by bad language, bad behaviour and the unfortunate quality in some of the young who think that to be brash, immoral and phoney Bohemian gives them the right to mix on equal terms with someone like Lesley.

This romantic lady has spurred me on to continue this book, giving me hints as to how to go about it. It has been a great help. 'Jot down in a notebook – a notebook that you carry everywhere, anything that comes to mind. The mind is so fickle that, if you don't, it will fly away, never to return.'

Lesley lives in the South of France near the Italian frontier. Both Gavin and I tried hard to persuade her to join us in Tangier. I think she would like to make the move, but as she was married to a Frenchman, the financial difficulties with the French authorities are overwhelming. All the same, we still have hopes.

Pauline Ab Yberg, born in Tangier of a Swiss father and Florentine mother, lived with them and a younger sister opposite the Menebhi Palace near the entrance to the Casbah. Madame Ab Yberg was an invalid. When I first met Pauline, she was working with Feridah Green at the Infant Welfare Centre which she took over after Feridah's death and ran superbly. I remember Pauline wheeling her mother around in a Bath chair in the summer evenings – a truly good and dutiful daughter. Her father had business in Geneva so he was seldom here.

Pauline was elegant, tall and thin. Her face radiated a sense of beauty. Her hair was dark, her black eyes sparkled with interest, her skin was like alabaster, and she had beautiful tapering fingers always exquisitely manicured. In every way her appearance was immaculate, and though far from rich she managed to appear so. Her clothes were in perfect taste and just right for every occasion. She spoke, read and wrote Italian, English, Spanish, French, German and Arabic with equal ease. She should have been an ambassadress and nearly was, for she was engaged to a diplomat in the American Legation; but the engagement was broken off. Obviously he was unable to resist the Ab Yberg family, for he later married her younger sister.

Until a few years ago Pauline had never travelled, even in Morocco, but with her avid reading of magazines and listening to people's conversation, she was brilliant enough to make one feel that she had not only attended all the great balls given in London, Paris, New York, Venice and Rome, but was an intimate friend of the hosts and hostesses. She was an outstanding personality in Tangier. She had strong likes and dislikes, and was influenced by nobody. She had many Moroccan friends, and having been born here, she had a complete understanding of the Moorish mentality and the many small nuances which we miss. This made Pauline one of them. She was immensely popular and we were lucky to have her working for us in the Infant Welfare Centre. She was as at home with the mothers, aunts, sisters and cousins who passed through our clinic as she would have been with any European equivalent. I have many Moroccan friends, but I envied her for the intimate contact she had with them.

Pauline had great courage. For instance, when I was standing in the pouring rain holding her hand as we watched the building in which she had her two-room apartment, containing everything she owned in the world, steadily burning with great tongues of flames creeping towards the top floor where her flat was situated, she did not flinch, she did not cry. She remained completely calm and silent, perhaps praying, I do not know, but I feel this calm came from the Arab philosophy 'Mektoub' (it is written). She lost everything.

Pauline started working for the Infant Welfare Centre when she was a very young girl. On her twenty-fifth anniversary of superintending the clinic, I called a meeting of the committee at the British Consulate to suggest that a generous present should be given her for the splendid work she had done and was still doing. It was agreed by a show of hands, and when we handed her the cheque, she said, 'Oh thank, thank you. My dream has come true. I can now buy myself a rope of cultured pearls.' I loved Pauline for that, as at the time she needed the money badly. Since then relations of hers died and Pauline became much better off, but she didn't live long to enjoy it. When she too died, the Spanish Cathedral was packed with people of every religion and nationality. It was a truly moving ceremony.

Before Independence it was impossible for a Moroccan woman to play any part in public life. The men expected them to stay at home, tend the children and run the house. Since then, however, the young educated Moroccan man is much more sophisticated and open-minded. There is one important fact, however, that every European woman should realize before making up her mind to marry a Muslim. The children must be brought up in their father's faith. There is no need for the wife to change her beliefs, but she must understand in advance the importance Muslims attach to their religion. There is a great similarity between our religions. We both worship the same God, but Muslims believe in the sayings of Muhammad the Prophet, and we in the sayings of Jesus Christ. It should not be difficult to reconcile the two ways of thought if you genuinely love your husband and family. As old Feridah Green used to say when discussing religion with her Muslim friends, 'Muhammad took on where Christ left off.'

Although it was customary to have more than one wife in the old days, it is much rarer now. Certainly none of my Muslim friends has more than one wife, and I am sure that little by little it will die a natural death, if only for financial reasons. It is hard enough to support one woman and her family, let alone two or three, so I do not feel that a European girl, if she chooses a decent man, should have the fear of being pushed aside to make way for another wife.

Hamid Nuamani, a Moroccan friend, told me that when he was a child, he was sent to the French Lycée in Fez. There were only four Moroccan students in a class of thirty-five children – French, Spanish and Jewish. The Moroccan children were admitted only because their father held some government post. He says they were always made to sit at the back of the class, and when they shone or did better than the European students, the schoolmaster was angry and would think up some other way of making them feel inferior.

Hamid comes from an ancient Berber tribe in the Middle Atlas. His family history has been handed down from father to son by word of mouth, as no written Berber language exists. The story goes that the father of the family living in the Middle Atlas many centuries ago did not approve of his eldest son's bride to be, who was considered unsuitable. Thus, the son left the tribe with his bride and settled far away in another part of the Atlas. Their children in turn grew up and married and had children, so little by little a township sprang up comprised of Hamid's ancestors, who lived on tilling the land and breeding animals useful to the existence of man. One of Hamid's ancestors about 350 years ago decided to exploit his produce and become a merchant. His land produced wool, leather, corn, fruit, olives and grain. Fez, which was the largest business centre of Morocco, was not far away, so he decided to buy land and build a second house for his business there. He moved his family and educated his children in the Koranic School. Hamid's family has lived there ever since.

Hamid was explaining to me the legal side of the Berber tribes in the old days. For instance, if a boy wounded or killed another, he would be taken by the headman of his village to the family of the victim. 'Here he is,' the headman would say. 'He is yours to do with as you wish. If you are compassionate, fine. If you are not, equally all right.' This very much resembles the Old Testament's 'eye for eye, tooth for tooth, hand for hand, foot for foot'. If a robber was caught, his right hand was cut off, since it is the most likely hand with which to steal. Left-handed thieves were therefore a little luckier.

Many years ago Tennessee Williams stayed at the Hotel Fahar on the Old Mountain, as did Truman Capote, Paul Bowles, Jack Dumphy and other writers and painters. They rented bungalows which were detached from the main building. Tennessee returned to Tangier several times since those days, but sadly he had become alcoholic. In spite of this he remained as nice as ever.

One evening at York Castle Tennessee arrived very drunk. As you enter the Castle you come into a lovely classical Moorish courtyard open to the sky. The courtyard is paved with ornamental tiles, and in the centre of it is a swimming-pool lined with the same tiles. Yves, our host, was standing at the far end receiving his guests, when Tennessee walked straight into the pool, thinking it was part of the courtyard. It is not deep and, quite unmoved, he walked the whole length of the pool, climbed out, shook hands with Yves and remained dripping from the waist down for the remainder of the evening.

I sometimes feel closer to my Moroccan friends than I do to my European acquaintances. This is partly because they have a sense of the ridiculous as well as a sense of humour. The French, Spanish and Italians are for the most part lacking in the former. Witty, amusing, intelligent and erudite as they are, they don't laugh at simple things, such as when someone slips up on banana peel or tries to open a glass door when it is already open, or steps into a shallow basin of water, as did Tennessee Williams. This sort of incident provokes laughter from the Moroccans – and the British too – but tongue-clicking from the French.

Another quality of the Moroccans that I enjoy is their love of teasing, which they do so subtly that not until they have you really worked up, do they let you into the joke. The same atmosphere exists when one is bargaining in a shop. The vendors quote the most ridiculously high prices, not intending them to be accepted, but if by chance some unsuspecting tourist agrees, they are delighted. Rocking with suppressed laughter, they will offer mint tea and almond cakes, winking at each other behind the back of the gullible customer. In spite of being pleased at the transaction, however, they are also disappointed that no haggling has occurred, for bargaining is the breath of life of the shopkeeper. I invariably offer just under half what they are asking, and usually end up by getting the object for just over half the original price. These transactions sometimes continue for any time up to an hour. Then, if neither buyer nor seller is satisfied, the buyer leaves the shop, to be followed a few minutes later by the seller, who meanwhile, rather than miss the sale, has decided to accept the offer. This method of shopping is like playing a game; they enjoy it themselves, and after living here so many years, so do I.

Owing to the teachings of Muhammad the Prophet, Muslim hospitality is recognized the world over. You may drop in at any hour of the day or night, and you are sure to be offered food and drink. Often I visit friends, the Oueslatis, who are my neighbours. They are an enchanting couple, intelligent and sympathetic. If I call in about midday, I am always asked to remain for lunch. Many times when I have been there, other friends have arrived and they are also asked to remain and eat. There always seems to be enough food prepared for any amount of uninvited guests. This hospitality is a tradition that has lasted for many centuries, and I am sure it will continue until the end of time.

Another quality that I have learned and admire about the Moroccans is their patience. Time is unimportant to them. This is evident in their everyday life. Nothing is done in a hurry. If whatever they are doing doesn't go right the first time, the second time, or even the third time, it is immaterial, because it is Allah's will. For instance, if an unfinished house they have been working on for weeks falls down owing to a storm, with a shrug of the shoulders they will calmly start all over again. If the telephone doesn't work, it doesn't work – that is all there is to it. Over the years I have developed the same way of thinking. It is now (at the time of writing) three weeks since I have had a telephone and, truthfully, I don't miss it. When fate decrees that I shall have a telephone, I shall have one. I suppose over a period of time I have adapted myself to the tempo of life here, but it comes as a shock when my visiting friends from Europe point this out to me.

The following story demonstrates the height of Moroccans' good manners.

Some years ago, Marguerite and James McBey had been invited to dinner with the Menebhi family at eight o'clock. They were bringing two visitors who were arriving that day. The boat was late and they did not arrive at the Menebhi Palace until nine o'clock. As they entered, the many grandfather clocks in the big reception-room all struck eight.

James McBey, the greatest etcher of this century, was a Scotsman of humble origin. He had ice-blue eyes, a mane of white hair, a gentle rather shy smile, and was the best raconteur to whom I have ever listened. Though famous for his etchings, he was in fact a fine water-colourist and a first-rate portrait painter in oils. He lived here for many years with his beautiful wife Marguerite.

Marguerite is American, with apricot skin, hair as blue-black as a raven's wing, finely drawn arched eyebrows and a neck like a swan. She has become one of my closest friends. She adored her husband and entirely subjugated herself to the Master. She was a great deal younger than James, and after he died proved herself to be an exceptionally good painter. Her water-colours are inspired, and she is planning an exhibition in New York.

Marguerite is beautifully dressed. She affects a style of her own and never follows fashion. Full skirts, usually long, shirts of different colours worn with silk scarves around her neck interwoven with pearls or sapphires, depending on the colour of the scarves – her sense of colour is superb and as unexpected as her beauty. When she removes her jewels at night, they are hung on a plastic tree – emeralds, sapphires and pearls glittering for all to see. It is a clever idea, as a thief would probably mistake them thus displayed for costume jewellery.

Marguerite is quite incapable of making up her mind without mulling over the situation for some days. This, I think, stems from her years of marriage with James. He decided everything, so it was not necessary for her to make decisions. When he died, she had to start again from the beginning. For instance, James would invite people only for 'high tea'. This was the final meal of the day, so the McBeys did not give dinner parties. James disliked going out, so rarely did they appear at luncheon parties. When they travelled James made the plans, and Marguerite carried them out. So being independent was a new experience for her when she became a widow, and she was forced to remake her life in the way she wanted. It took some years for her to adjust to this unforeseen freedom, and to this day she hesitates. Should she or should she not go to a certain place? Should she or should she not allow an article on James to be published? What should she pack? Should she go to Vienna before London, or London before Vienna? And so on.

Two years ago Marguerite and I were going to Lebanon. We flew to Barcelona, whence we were to travel on a Turkish ship to Beirut. On arrival we were told that the civil war had started, the airports and seaports were closed, and our ship had been ordered to return passengerless to Istanbul. We were determined not to return to Tangier, having been told that we were mad to attempt our trip, as things were looking so bad in Lebanon. We dreaded the 'I told you so'.

After several delicious days eating oysters, strolling up and down the Ramblas looking at the booths which were filled with exotic birds, and smelling the flowers that lined the parade, we procured a flight to Athens via Rome. On our arrival, Marguerite's large suitcase was missing. We had spent hours together deciding what she should take and she was in despair, not only because of the clothes, but she had packed her jewellery in that particular suitcase. We sent telegrams, we demanded to see the director of Air Alitalia, we demanded to see the Ambassador. All to no avail. Suddenly Marguerite gave up the unequal struggle – and was superb. She bought two skirts, borrowed a few of my shirts which suited her to perfection, and never enjoyed a holiday more, chiefly, as she said, because 'I didn't have to decide what to wear, for I had no choice.'

Her problem of indecision was solved the hard way. The suitcase was found at Rome airport six months later.

Athens was crowded with people, primarily Americans who were rerouted from the Middle East. Accommodation was at first impossible, so we went to Delphi where we spent three days. Marguerite painted some lovely water-colours and bought one embroidered skirt for evenings. On returning to Athens we found good rooms in the Palace Hotel. We did the usual sightseers' tour and spent one day on an excursion steamer visiting three or four islands. Marjorie Tweeddale joined us and we flew to Crete and on to Rhodes and Corfu, where we boarded an Italian ship bound for Venice. Patrick Thursfield joined us there and motored Marjorie and me to Genoa, where there happened to be a canary show. We all bought, and our cabins on the boat taking us to Malaga were aviaries, with singing birds and birdseed all over the floor. The stewards were sympathetic. I had bought more than the others, but my steward was a bird-fancier and bred canaries in Malaga.

We took another boat to Tangier, and on arrival the Moroccan Customs officer said, 'Please show me their vaccination certificates.' For the moment we thought he was serious; then, on seeing our horrified faces, he burst into laughter and waved us on.

We are spoilt in Tangier, for in many ways we are still able to lead the same kind of life as we did before the last war. Willing servants are available, and as they have no feeling of inferiority, servility does not exist. The Moroccans have great pride and very little class consciousness, so if you treat them as friends or part of the family, the atmosphere in the house is extremely happy.

Mohammed, my cook, and the others who work for me, love parties and are disappointed if I don't have many house guests during the year. They say, 'When is your sister coming? When is your cousin coming? When are all your nephews and nieces coming?' Added to this, they are so welcoming when my guests do arrive that it makes their visits that much nicer. It is a splendid rest for my friends and relations from England, who live mostly without help of any kind, to come here and wallow in what I hope is luxury, and be looked after with loving care by my faithful Mohammed, Fatima and Noureddine.

The Moroccans are instinctively good cooks. When my Spanish cook retired to Spain, I said to Mohammed, then my gardener, 'Now we've got to find a new cook. Do you know of anyone?'

'Yes,' he replied. 'Me.'

'You, Mohammed? But I had no idea you were a cook.'

'I am not, señor, but I've watched Antonio for ten years. If you give me a chance, I'm sure I shall be just as good as he was.'

'All right, we'll give it a try. Go ahead.' This happened several years ago, and he has turned out to be much better than Antonio ever was.

My new gardener is young and efficient. He is named Ali. He loves the garden and flowers. He arrived one morning with a bunch for me, probably pinched from a neighbour's garden.

'Oh, thank you, Ali,' I said, shaking my finger at him. 'Where did you get these from?'

'Allah, señor,' he replied.

A few months ago I was sitting in the Café de Paris with some friends. We were discussing Morocco and King Hassan. One member of the party was having his shoes cleaned by a ten-year-old shoeshine boy who was listening to our conversation. He said to me, 'I know, Mr David, that you love Morocco and Monsieur Hassan II and I hope your friends do too.' With that, he put down his brushes, stood up and said, 'Monsieur Hassan II est un homme remarquable, et personne ne peut le tuer sauf Allah.'

This story shows the deep loyalty and affection that even the children of Morocco have for their king.

When I first came to live in Tangier, you rarely saw a Moroccan with a dog as a pet. Dogs were used only as guards for their houses. In recent years, more and more Moroccans have a dog as a friend. Frequently, in Tangier and elsewhere, you see a man or woman with a well-fed, well-groomed dog on a lead. This is a welcome sight to any animal lover.

The Moroccans have always liked cats. They respect them because, so history relates, Muhammad the Prophet fell asleep in the countryside and woke up to find a cat asleep on his djellaba. Rather than disturb the sleeping animal, he cut out the piece of cloth on which the cat was lying.

It is forbidden here by law to trap wild birds, but that does not stop the boys in the country from doing so. During the migrating season many different kinds of birds pass through Tangier – golden orioles, blue rollers, hoopoes, butcher-birds, bee-eaters, to name some. The easiest to catch are the butcher-birds because they nest in low, stubbly bushes. On the road to Cap Spartel in April you find boys with four or five of these birds, each with a feather pushed through the nostrils of its beak, and tied by the legs to a piece of string. The boys wave these wretched birds as though they were kites at passing cars to attract attention. Unfortunately people stop to buy them, sometimes to eat, sometimes to release them. The more they are bought, the more the boys try to catch them to gain a few more dirhams.

A few years ago I passed two of these boys with about a dozen butcher-birds. I stopped the car, pretending I wanted to buy them. I told the boys to get in the car with the birds and I would pay them. The moment they were inside, I accelerated and said, 'I am taking you straight to the police station, but if you remove the feathers from their beaks and release their legs, I will ask the police to be lenient.'

The boys were frightened and did as I told them. The result was that I arrived at the police station with two terrified youngsters and the wild birds mad with fear. They had been flying about inside the car squeaking and leaving their droppings all over the seats, crashing against the windscreen and almost blinding me, making it virtually impossible to drive. The policemen, on seeing this extraordinary sight, burst into gales of laughter, for which I did not blame them. Then they pulled themselves together, took the boys, gave them a thorough beating, and made them walk ten miles back to their homes. The birds flew away, and the policemen and I went to the café next door and had some coffee.

The authorities are doing their best to prevent the trapping of birds, but it is practically impossible to patrol the whole countryside. Even so, I notice that each year there are fewer boys on the side of the roads selling them. I imagine, with the higher standard of living and education, that before long the practice will die out altogether.

The migrating season is a fascinating period for me as a bird lover. Because of the aviaries in my garden, the wild birds are attracted by the chatter and the food, so it is full of hoopoes, orioles and rollers. The butcher-birds never appear, for what reason I do not know. Last year I had a plague of sparrows, which not only ate all the buds off my wisteria, but mobbed the migratory birds when they flew into the garden. This year I bought a shotgun; the wisteria is blooming and the wild birds are back in the garden.

Joe McPhillips, the good-looking Headmaster of the American School of Tangier, is a dedicated teacher. He has lived here many years, in fact since the new American School of Tangier was built. I remember the old one from the day it opened some forty years ago in the Rue Alexandria, now renamed Hassan II. It was then a small day school for the children of American nationals working here. Over the years it has steadily progressed and become a thriving concern. It is expanding each year. The mixture of races and creeds in the only English-speaking school in Tangier is remarkable.

Two hundred years ago the Kingdom of Morocco was the first country to recognize the independence of America when she seceded from Great Britain in the reign of George III. It is splendid to think that today the friendship between the three countries is so closely knit. Every year more children from all parts of the world come to this school to receive their education and to make friends with people of other religions and nationalities. I feel that this unique school is an example of what can be done when people are truly dedicated, for through it a new feeling of respect and understanding for other people's way of life is emerging. I hope that the sense of comradeship found in this school may prove a forerunner to a happier and more peaceful world for those children who will shortly leave to face the difficult and tumultuous times in which we live.

Joe has just returned from a whirlwind tour of black Africa where he has succeeded, through his untiring energy and determination, in enrolling forty more students. In consequence, the dormitory will be full to overflowing in the year ahead.

When Joe was a junior master, he was in charge of the school theatrical group. Each year he produced a classic of some sort, either a Greek tragedy or a Shakespeare play. He is an excellent director and what he got out of this mixture of students was extraordinary. He invariably asked me to read the prologue, dressed in a black cape and wearing Roman sandals. The reasons for this was that many of the parents understood very little English and it was supposed that mine was more understandable than most. In a precise and unnatural voice I would explain what the play was about. It was a difficult and unrewarding role. I would stand alone on the stage, with the spotlight focused on me, and start speaking to a stone-cold audience, barely a quarter of whom, I am sure, understood what I was talking about. I did this out of affection for Joe, but, unbeknown to me, I discovered that it made him unpopular with the stuffy members of the board of directors who in those days were insular and considered any Englishman cashing in on their school an interloper.

All this has changed; the board now are young, go-ahead, and totally without prejudice. They have invited me to write an article in their next year's brochure, and also to decorate a common-room in the Moroccan style for the living-in students.

A year or so ago Joe produced two of Jane Bowles's short stories, which he had dramatized himself. *Camp Cataract* and *The Puppet Play*. Both were complicated and highly sophisticated works but, oddly enough, the young students who acted in them understood the plays at once. Not so the parents. All Janie's works were thirty years ahead of the times, and for this reason Joe asked me to explain to the audience the theme before each play: a sort of prologue written beautifully by Joe himself. This I did with pleasure, but whether the parents understood the plays any better I shall never know. It was a successful venture and nostalgic for me, reminding me of the long speeches I had made before the grand productions years ago.

Janie's true fame came after her early death. She was a perfectionist and was seldom satisfied with what she had written. Alas, because of this, comparatively little of her work remains.

During the International Zone period we presented yearly productions for the benefit of local charities and made a great deal of money. After Independence, many people left and the theatrical activities died a natural death. Some years ago they were restarted by Robert Eliot, an Englishman living here. At that time I had nothing to do with the rebuilding of the Tangier Theatre, but a few years ago Richard Timewell, the retired furniture expert from Sotheby's, became president and asked me to join. I was pleased and flattered, saying I would help in any way possible on the production side but that I didn't want to act again after so many years of retirement.

I was producing *Red Peppers* by Noël Coward when the man who was playing the theatre manager in the play had a heart attack. I was forced to take his place at the last moment. Since then I have been persuaded to appear in what I know I am best doing – a grotesque woman's part. I always played an ugly sister or the dame in our pantomimes, so I was thought suitable for the theatre's next production. This was to be called *An Evening of Laughter and Fun*, a variety show. One of the numbers was a scene from *Lady Windermere's Fan* by Oscar Wilde. I played the Duchess of Berwick, supported by Brenda Gerolemou and Richard Millard, both excellent actors. Many people still living here remembered me in the pantomime days and were loyal enough to be pleased that after all this time I was making a 'come-back'.

When I made my first appearance for many years, I was taken aback and deeply flattered by the wonderful applause and warmth of the audience. This put me on my mettle and I gave, I think, a creditable performance. The critics in the local papers were kind and gave me much confidence, so that I was prepared to accept other roles if I was asked.

Recently I played the part of Henry VIII's surviving wife, Catherine Parr, in an amazingly funny playlet by Maurice Baring. The American Consul-General Hal Eastman played the King. Henry is an old man and Catherine a young woman. They are depicted having breakfast in the palace. The play consists of their bickering like any ordinary couple, starting with whether the eggs have been properly boiled or not, and continuing in the same vein as to whether Alexander the Great's horse was black or white, and ending with their insulting each other's family. Henry loses his temper and sends for the executioner, but in the end he relents. It is a flimsy piece, but since it was done as a twenty-minute sketch in a cabaret, it was successful and caused a great deal of laughter.

The Tangier Theatre no longer exists but it served a dual purpose. It existed not only for entertaining, but as a get-together for people of vastly opposite ways of life. You saw the most unlikely people kissing each other good-night. This was a particularly good thing in Tangier, for there was no club or meeting-place where the British community could gather.

The Tangier branch of the PDSA (People's Dispensary for Sick Animals), of which I was chairman, was started sixty years ago and has done splendid work amongst the animals owned by poor Moroccans who earn their livelihood from beasts of burden. You rarely see donkeys with sores on their backs or horses with wounds on their sides, because the Moroccans have learned from the PDSA how to look after them. They are not wilfully cruel, but in the early days they did not seek medical help, as it was non-existent. Now the Moroccans flock to our clinic in the Rue San Francisco. They leave their animals with us and return in a week or so to collect them, usually cured from whatever ailment they were suffering. It is rewarding to see the look of joy and amazement on the faces of those who thought their cow, sheep, horse, mule or donkey would certainly die, and then find it fat, glossy and bright-eyed.

Ernest Preston, our veterinary superintendent, was totally dedi-cated to his work. He would get up any time of night to tend a sick cow, a bitch having puppies or any animal seriously ill. He had been working in Tangier for twenty-five years and the time came for him to retire. This was a cruel blow, as he was irreplaceable, being respected and loved by Moroccans and Europeans alike.

We held an annual bazaar in the garden of the British Consu-late. At this function we made a profit of over £1,000, which is remarkable in a small community like Tangier. We had food-stalls, side-shows of every description, and a running bar as well as soft drinks and sandwiches. Towards the end of the evening I used to get up on a rostrum and auction a dozen or so objects of a certain value which had been given us by local people, and any bottles of drink or iced cakes that had not been sold at the stalls. It was an exhausting job, and I usually had no voice for a couple of day afterwards.

At our annual meeting to decide upon the events for the bazaar, we were pessimistic. Each year we said, 'Of course this year we shan't make so much money. People must be getting sick of the same thing over and over again.' But the generosity and loyalty of the local people is such that we were always proved wrong.

Ernest's successor, Donald Cousens, more than lived up to our expectations. He was with us for five or six years and retired last year. Sadly, the PDSA is also coming to an end. It was inevitable that one day this should happen, for in the years gone by there were no Moroccan vets because during the Protectorate they were French, in the Spanish Zone Spanish, and in the International Zone of Tangier, English. Now there are excellent Moroccan vets, and we have been taken over by SPANA – the Society for the

Protection of Animals in North Africa. It is an English concern but employs only Moroccan, Algerian and Tunisian vets.

The English Church of St Andrews' lovely cemetery is more of a garden than a cemetery and lies adjacent to the Moorish burial-ground. For many years Eva Lumb tended it with loving care, and in doing so created something unique. There is nothing municipal about it and the atmosphere of peace is remarkable. The church itself was built and endowed by Sir Jock Brooks about ninety years ago and is architecturally Moorish. It is a plain white building with a green-tiled roof and a Moorish tower instead of a spire. The inside is also white, with two lines of Moorish arches representing the side-aisles. There stands a great Moorish arch dividing the main body of the church from the transept, around which is written the Lord's Prayer in Arabic. The altar is of white marble, as also is the pulpit, which resembles an octagonal tower. The ceilings are of cedarwood, exquisitely painted in the traditional Moorish style.

Ninety years ago taste in England was represented by St Pancras Station and the like. We are lucky that Sir Jock Brooks had a different idea, or now there would probably stand a red-brick Victorian monster totally unsuited to the surroundings.

Tangier is a difficult place for a vicar. Since I have been consular churchwarden, which is well over twenty years, we have had no fewer than nine clergymen – some good, some indifferent. The petty squabbles and backbiting in the community, however, have been too much for them. They could not stand it for more than a year or so. One poor man even took his life while ministering here.

One of their most difficult jobs is visiting the prison, which is always crowded with European hippies arrested for drug smuggling. Many are English and unless their families pay a large fine they remain there indefinitely.

Very few of the young Moroccans whom I know smoke kif, but there is a thriving business in the Rif Mountains where it is grown. Boys run out of the woods to sell it to passing European tourists, who buy quantities to take back to their respective countries and resell at a vast price. They are usually caught by the Customs at the airport or the seaport as they are leaving Morocco, and clapped into prison.

In all village life the church plays an important part. Tangier is no exception: our local church is a centre for the Anglican community, some Americans and a few Protestant French. A smattering of Orthodox Russians and Greeks also attend St Andrews. The last few years there has been an unpleasant series of events connected with the church. One of our most respected elderly ladies said to me, 'There is an evil spirit going around this church.' I myself received an anonymous letter of such nastiness that it was hard to imagine the poor twisted mind that wrote it. Moreover, it was placed in the offertory bag. On opening the letter, I took it to the vicar, Basil Kitchen, who was disgusted by its contents. As he was new here, he did not realize that I was able to take this sort of thing in my stride. He was distressed for me. I told him not to worry and that I was going to broadcast it all over the town.

I also told him that when I was about fourteen years old, I was sitting with my mother in her boudoir when the post was brought in. Amongst the letters there was a small parcel. My mother opened it. Inside was a Cartier jewel case. 'Who could be sending me jewels?' my mother said. She lifted the lid and inside lay a small cowpat. I was horrified, as any son would be, and felt how terrible she must be feeling. She saw the expression on my face and laughed, saying, 'Don't worry, darling, I've had this sort of thing happen to me before. You must pity the poor, unhappy, bitter and resentful people who send them.' She then rang for her faithful maid, Miss Baker, and said, 'Look, aren't we lucky! You know that Cartier case which holds the big sapphire brooch His Lordship gave me some years ago? Well, it's falling to bits. Now we can throw it away. Just have this one cleaned and we can use it instead.'

'So don't worry about me, Basil, I shall take it the way mother did.'

The following Sunday I was taken unawares when Basil came to the centre of the church and said, 'A member of this congregation has received the most disgusting and outrageous anonymous letter. I am sixty-eight years old, and I assure you that the contents of this letter are the most sickening piece of slander that I have ever read in the whole of my life as a vicar. I want you all to get on your knees and pray for the soul of the person who wrote it. He or she has defiled the house of God by putting this missive in the offertory bag. Pray, therefore, that they may be forgiven by Almighty God.'

A certain member of the congregation wept.

The British Consulate is now closed, which is a great loss not only to us but for the British Navy when stationed in Gibraltar, for they have nowhere else in the vicinity to spend their leave, except on the Rock itself. As everyone knows, Gibraltar is a small promontory jutting out into the sea; there are virtually no beaches and no drives, and there is almost nothing to do there. Thanks to these deficiencies, Tangier was a haven for the Royal Navy. We had two or three ships, destroyers, frigates and submarines arriving every few months. This was a strain on the British Consulate, as the Consul-General had to entertain them on an inadequate entertainment allowance from the Foreign Office. Nevertheless, he did it magnificently. Added to this, the smartness and good behaviour of the officers and men were excellent publicity for us amongst the Moroccans. All this has changed since the opening of the frontier between Gibraltar and Spain, making things much easier for a lot of people.

Before Gibraltar obtained self-government, after the plebiscite in 1967 to decide whether it would remain under the British Crown, Tangier residents of all nationalities, including Moroccans, visited the Rock to do their shopping. In those days it was a free port and therefore infinitely cheaper than anywhere else. Gone are those halcyon days, for Gibraltar is no longer a free port. Since it is not self-supporting, the necessities of life, as well as luxuries, have to be imported. Inevitably it has become more expensive. Personally, I didn't bother to shop there because by the time you paid your air-fare there and back, your hotel bills, your meals, your taxis and tips, you had gained nothing – unless you are unable to exist without kippers, sausages and ham.

Ceuta, the Spanish possession opposite Gibraltar on the African mainland, has now taken the place of Gibraltar. You can drive there for the day, as it is only sixty miles from Tangier. Goods are cheap, if indifferent, and as travelling expenses are low, it does contribute some saving in your shopping.

However, neither of these places has tourist attractions, though recently Gibraltar has again come into its own, owing to the falling of the pound. In Gibraltar the English pound is still worth a pound, which it isn't when changed into other foreign currencies. Thus the English tourists can have a holiday in the sun without being out of pocket. It is amusing to think that both places (the two 'Pillars of Hercules') – Gibraltar belonging to Britain on the tip of the Spanish mainland, and Ceuta belonging to Spain on the tip of the Moroccan mainland – have each in turn had their day.

For many years I cherished a hope that the Queen would visit Morocco. This hope was realized in November 1980 when she and the Duke of Edinburgh arrived on a state visit. The welcome she received was tremendous. I had the honour to be invited to lunch with her in Rabat at the Palais des Hôtes, where she was staying. This small palace was built by King Hassan for the sole use of visiting heads of state. The architecture is classical Moroccan and it is decorated in perfect taste. The flower arrangements in the palace for the Queen's visit were remarkable. Tubs of several different species of orchids graced the entrance hall, whilst bowls of roses and jasmine were displayed on every table in the reception-room. On the dining-room table were low, oblong vases consisting of sprays of pink cymbidium orchids mixed with every variety of protea. In a mosaic alcove in the same room was an eight-foot-high pyramid built of giant strelitzias and flame-coloured bougainvillaea.

The Queen, lovely in a turquoise blue and white chiffon dress and coat with a turban of the same material, looked fresh and incredibly young. How she manged to do so after a gruelling tour of Italy, Tunisia and Algeria prior to coming here, I cannot imagine. She had arrived by plane from Algiers that morning and had shaken hands with several hundred officials and dignitaries at the airport. She was then driven, standing up in an open car with King Hassan beside her, through cheering crowds for ten miles. On arrival at the main square in Rabat, the procession halted whilst the two monarchs left the car and the Queen received the traditional welcome of almond milk and dates. They then proceeded to the Palais des Hôtes for lunch. Owing to vast crowds and unexpected delays, they were already behind schedule, so the lunch-break was short. The Queen, determined to stick to her programme, sent back several courses.

Directly lunch was finished, she drove to lay a wreath at the tomb of King Hassan's father, Mohammed V. From there she went to the British Embassy for a garden reception given by the Ambassador, Simon Dawbarn (whom she knighted at the end of her visit), to meet 180 British residents in Morocco, many of whom had married Moroccans. The Queen and Prince Philip spoke to each person individually and captured the hearts of all. I wish they could have heard the eulogies of praise after they had left.

By this time it was 4.30 p.m., though the day's activities were far from over. The next item on the programme was a visit to the Parliament building, where the Queen delivered a speech. After this, there was another reception given for the diplomatic corps. In the evening the King gave a banquet in her honour.

The visit was to last three days, with side-trips to Marrakesh, Fez and Casablanca. How the Queen got through that first day, always smiling and interested, I don't know, but I do know that there is no one in the world who works harder and is more dedicated to her job than she is. The whole world looks up to her and we, the British people, should ever be proud and grateful to her.

INDEX